D0429951

San Antonio
22 December 1998

ENCOUNTERS

Encounters

Edited by Kai Erikson

YALE UNIVERSITY PRESS   NEW HAVEN & LONDON

Designed by Richard Hendel
and set in Palatino type
by Capital City Press, Montpelier, Vermont.
Printed in the United States of America by
Vail-Ballou Press, Binghamton, New York.

Library of Congress catalog card number: 89-50863
International standard book number: 0-300-04662-6

The paper in this book meets the guidelines for
permanence and durability of the Committee on
Production Guidelines for Book Longevity of the
Council on Library Resources.

10 9 8 7 6 5 4 3 2

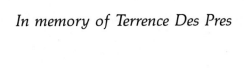

In memory of Terrence Des Pres

CONTENTS

INTRODUCTION

Ralph Kirkpatrick once showed me the draft of a memoir he had hoped
to publish with a chapter entitled "Assignments and Encounters"— sketches
of some of the more interesting people he had come into contact with over
the years. *The Yale Review*, of which I was then editor, printed the two
longest of those sketches in the summer of 1982, one on Paul Hindemith
and the other on Igor Stravinsky. They were wonderful, both of them. But
I was even more taken by some of the briefer fragments Kirkpatrick had
tucked in between the formal portraits, including a one-paragraph description of the afternoon Billie Holiday had been brought to his apartment to
hear him play Bach. Kirkpatrick doubted that Holiday had ever heard of
Bach, and the harpsichord (if that was what he played that day) could
hardly have been a very familiar instrument to her. But he remembered
her as one of the most intelligent listeners he had ever met. As "she put
away the better part of a bottle of rum," he wrote, "her face registered
everything; no manifestation of the music seemed to escape her . . . I
could have used her like an infinitely sensitive precision instrument to
monitor my performance of the G minor English Suite" simply by
watching "the subtle variations of expression on her face."

We wanted to print a few of those fragments, too, but Kirkpatrick was
unwilling for us to do so. They would not stand on their own as memoirs,
he thought; they were fleeting, insubstantial, without narrative form. But
they are certainly *encounters*, I pleaded, and anything going by such a
name can be judged by another standard, no? Alas, no. So I lost the argu-
ment but not the idea that had started it.

Autobiography, William Zinsser notes, "moves in a dutiful line from birth to fame, omitting nothing significant," while the "writer of a memoir takes us back to a corner of his or her life that was unusually vivid or intense." A memoir is not a life, then, or even a scrap lifted from a life in the same way that one might extract a passage from a text. It is "a window into a life"—a telling glance, a reflection, a moment of special meaning. Now Zinsser is speaking here of autobiographical memoirs by way of introducing a handful of them (*Inventing the Truth: The Art and Craft of Memoir*, 1987), but the same could be said of the kinds of memoir to be found in the collection to follow—each a brief profile drawn from the writer's own personal experience.

An encounter is for the most part "about" someone else, as the titles of all the ones presented here would suggest, and the pages to follow offer some wonderful glances at those other persons. A voice:

He spoke in a curiously strangled voice, with gaps between his sentences, as if ideas jostled and thrashed about inside him, getting in each other's way as they struggled to emerge, which made for short bursts, emitted staccato, interspersed with gentle, low-voiced, legato passages. [Berlin on Wilson]

A visage:

Next, piercing pale blue eyes, the bluer for being lashed into the pink face of a redhead. Thinning light-red hair, ill-brushed and tufted, over a wide dome of a forehead. Then, in better focus, terrible cheeks, riddled, ravaged, and pitted . . . Narrow, dry lips, and a slender chin. I would have sworn that he was hideously ugly until he started to talk, when his face suddenly turned on, like a delicate, brilliant lamp. [Hersey on Lewis]

A bearing:

His reaction to the music was physical. He was dapper and neat to look at, and arranged in straight lines; but the body moved in curves as if compelled from deep within. [Yeston on Lerner]

A mood:

I recall here the moment of Austin's response . . . a moment I de-

scribed as of spiritual perfection. The eyes that had been fixed wide
with attention were now almost closed, and wrinkled at the corners,
with satisfaction; the lips were pursed as if to keep from letting forth
laughter; and the pipe came back up, the tip not quite to the mouth
but to be punched lightly and repeatedly against the chin. Here was
serious mirth in progress. [Cavell on Austin]

A prose style:

But once in that milieu she loved, of funky houses not quite fallen
from grace, endlessly slipper-easy kitchen-table conversations, and
ideas siphoning like fungi through what a minute ago was a domestic
scene, she could bring you the soul and smell of wherever she chose.
[Calisher on Stead]

In a very real sense, however, an encounter is an event in the life of the
person writing rather than an event in the life of the person being written
about. It has its location, as it were, in the landscape of the writer's own
life. So it should be no surprise that the writers of these pieces so often
place themselves at or near the center of the scenes they are describing.
John Hollander begins his account of W. H. Auden by recalling Auden's
injunction, "When you write of something or someone don't talk about
yourself." That gives Hollander real pause, for it is no easy matter to "stay
invisible" when your own memory is the only source of information you
can draw on. When your own experience must serve as the solvent in
which the particulars of another's experience fuse and take definition.
When the trajectories of your own life have to provide whatever narrative
logic the account you are writing is likely to have.

This is true in more than one respect.

Even when an encounter cannot reasonably be said to have had an impact on the life of the teller—Quentin Bell's meeting with Henri Matisse
and Paul Horgan's with Mary Garden being good cases in point—the
figure being portrayed clearly belongs to, is a creature of, the younger
person in whose memory the event was originally registered. It is not a
measured likeness, not a portrait for history. Bell's Matisse—an "amiable
philistine" who could easily have passed as a wine merchant—is drawn in
the disappointed strokes of the young man who expected to encounter a
"gigantic" spirit, a "deity." And the Mary Garden we meet in Paul Horgan's

sketch is a sly conjuror, an apparition of her own casting who helped the
dazzled and playful young man he remembers himself as having been
more than half a century ago create a scene "out of thin air."

Most encounters, though, have a special significance to those doing the
remembering. They are retained in memory and later retold not just because they provide a moment of insight into the persons depicted (although that is often their warrant for being written) but because they had
a shaping influence on the lives of the tellers. The nature of that influence
becomes an important strand of the story being told, even when the account itself focuses in a straightforward way on the persons being
portrayed—as is the case, say, in the essays by Calisher, Hersey, and
Rustin. But when people are invited to compose something called encounters, they are being invited to place themselves in the action, to describe the ways in which they were molded by it. Indeed, long stretches
of the accounts to follow consider moments when the ostensible subject
is not present at all, and in a number of them—the ones by Bok, Gray,
Ruff, Cavell, Hollander, Settle, and (in a way) Bruner, for instance—the
narrative continues long after its subject is dead or is no longer an active
part of the teller's life.

The lives of subject and teller, in fact, have a way of overlapping, of
folding into one another. Chronology supplies the organizing principle of
these essays, as is the case in all tales, but much of the narrative is viewed
backward, as if (Alva Myrdal's phrase) in a "rearview mirror." In all of
the encounters here reprinted, the rememberers were younger than the
persons remembered; but a number of them note in an almost puzzled way
that they are now substantially older than the individuals who then
seemed to them so grey and full of years. John Hersey was twenty-three
when he met the fifty-two-year-old Sinclair Lewis, but over seventy when
he recalled the meeting; Quentin Bell was twenty-four when he met
Matisse, then a "comfortably plump" man of sixty-five, but the teller of
that story is now approaching eighty. And the same is true, if less drasti-
cally so, in all but two or three of the memoirs to be found here. The
fathers, mothers, and children of those telling the tales, moreover, often
enter the scene and play a more than passing role in it, contributing to a
feeling that the flows of life have turned in on themselves and drawn the
world of the teller and the world of the subject into a setting outside those
"dutiful" linearities of time. The last words of Hollander's essay are about

his daughter in a time long after Auden's death; the last words of Cavell's essay are about his father in a time long before his protagonist, J. L. Austin, was born. So encounters can be framed by other boundaries, moved by other urgencies, than the lives of the individuals who occupy their centers.

The longest and closest association described here, for example, is that of Sissela Bok and her recently deceased mother, the great Alva Myrdal. The core of the memoir is an encounter between Bok, a distinguished writer of fifty, and a teenaged girl named Alva Reimer from a provincial town in Sweden who lived seventy years ago and would not become Alva Myrdal for another decade. Eight months after Alva's death at eighty-two, Sissela "heard that girl's voice" when a packet of letters by her mother, the first of them written in 1916, was delivered to her. So here was the daughter in her middle years, reading the words of the fourteen-year-old who would one day be her mother, "as near as if she sat across the table from me and young enough to be my daughter."

Francine Gray's account of her growth in the presence of Charles Olson, for another example, requires us to know at least something about her life before meeting Olson and a good deal about it afterward. The Francine du Plessix who presented her immensely gifted self to Olson's Black Mountain at twenty was the product of another time, and the true measure of Olson—a mentor, after all—ought to be how the presence of the teacher is reflected in the life and writings of the pupil. That, surely, is what makes this an encounter, a meeting of two vital spirits rather than the silhouette of some distant figure drawn from memory.

Mary Lee Settle, finally, tells us of Somerset Maugham at eighty—once a younger contemporary of James, Conrad, Wells, Kipling—and his meetings with a young writer about to publish her first novel. She was astonished by Maugham's grace and generosity in her first glimpse of him, so distant was the person from the reputation. But the second meeting left an impression so sharp and caustic that it continues to sting thirty-five years later. The cold, reptilian face that resides in Settle's memory, lined with suspicion and malice and pain, has had a prominent place in her thoughts through all the years of success that followed. Her encounter with Maugham was a crucial moral moment in her life, a recollection she draws out of the files in her mind "every two or three years" in order to immerse herself in it "like a necessary cold shower." The essay speaks volumes about Maugham, then, but its true subject, clearly, is both the young apprentice who was so repelled by his touch and the seasoned writer that apprentice became.

On the whole, these essays are not as reflective as one might suppose about the act of remembering — of recreating, reconstructing, inventing the past. Jerome Bruner, in contrast, who brings this collection to a close, writes of an unremarkable outing, a "day out of memory," in which nothing much happened other than a good conversation, a pleasant local wine, a fine trailside snack, and, of course, the company of Jean Piaget, whom everyone knew as Le Patron. Bruner sent a draft of his *Review* essay to Bärbel Inhelder, a longtime associate of Piaget's who had shared the modest adventures of that day. It was meant as a postcard, a greeting, a souvenir. But Bruner then received a telephone call from Geneva, where Inhelder still lives, to the effect that Bruner had misdated the outing by a matter of several years and that the occasion was in other respects quite different from his recollection of it. Inhelder — her own memory having been reinforced by the fourth person who had been present — noted that the most memorable event of the day had been a drenching thunderstorm, a happening that Bruner cannot now recover no matter how deeply he dredges the stuff of his unconscious. So what *is* an encounter? he then asks. From what inner reserves do its traces come? By what human chemistry are those traces linked into a narrative?

Well, it may not matter very much, and certainly not for our purposes here; but to speak of "encounters" rather than of "biographies" or "portraits" is to underscore an important point. The experiences on the basis of which one person draws the profile of another emanate from a scene that both of them helped make. The words a subject speaks, then, and the ways a subject acts cannot be understood simply as impulses welling up from within or as reflections of some inner self. They are emergent from that scene and, thus, a product of it. To know those surroundings, the context in which the story unfolds, is to know a larger truth.

Several years after the *Review* printed Kirkpatrick's profiles of Hindemith and Stravinsky, its editors sent out letters to a number of persons inviting them "to describe their experiences of someone of special note." These encounters, we noted, "may be chance meetings, long associations, even confrontations . . . They can be short, long, whimsical, respectful, but we are primarily interested in capturing glimpses of people no longer living while the memories of those who knew them remain fresh." As a result of those solicitations, thirty-two encounters appeared in our Winter 1987 and Spring 1987 issues, and another eleven, more than a year later, in Summer 1988. The present gathering of eighteen is drawn from those three issues. They were not sifted from the whole and declared "the best" in the manner of so many collections one finds on booksellers' shelves these days; they are a sampling that seem to us to fit well together.

My partners in the making of the *Review* "Encounters" issues were my fellow editors Penelope Laurans, J. D. McClatchy, and Wendy Wipprecht; my partner in the making of this book was John Ryden, director of Yale University Press. Together we owe special debts to Marie Borroff, Joanna Erikson, Jonathan Fanton, the late Robert Fitzgerald, John Hollander, and Maureen Howard.

Bayard Rustin died not long after his profile of A. Philip Randolph appeared in the *Review*. He was a very special person.

ENCOUNTERS

PAUL HORGAN

L'Après-midi de Mary Garden

On Tuesday morning, 29 January 1935, in New York, I awoke to a state of alarm mixed with elation. It was the publication day of *No Quarter Given*, my second novel, and Harper and Brothers were giving an all-out cocktail party for the occasion. In those days, the literary cocktail party was more of an event than it is now. All of New York's literary *gratin* turned out. Faces famous in caricature, minds tautly competitive, common charity disdained, the guests came to be seen and reported. The guest of honor was often said to be the least of the attractions. I had read all this in New Mexico, where I lived. Now about to be thrown in the thick of it, I thought how comfortable it would be simply to bolt. The dreadful day yawned ahead of me. How to get through it until five o'clock, when I must appear? Whenever the thought of the coming ordeal struck me, I felt the classic symptoms of stage fright—a tightening of the scalp, a thump at the solar plexus.

At breakfast, a sudden refuge in distraction faced me in the *New York Times*. There I found an item announcing that Mary Garden, the lustrous opera singer and actress, would present a lecture-recital in the Plaza Hotel ballroom at three o'clock that day. Her subject was Claude Debussy. Tickets could be had at a box office in the hotel. All my life—I was thirty-two—I had wanted to see and hear this amazing artist.

To mention Caruso, Melba, Farrar, Chaliapin, or, for today, Maria Callas, is to suggest the like position of Mary Garden in the international operatic world of her time. Much of her lore was known to me. I knew her voice through recordings. While still a vocal student in Paris she had won instant fame by brilliantly taking over the lead role in Charpentier's *Louise* when the artist singing the part became ill. On that night, Garden was established for life. She was twenty-six. Two years later Debussy chose her to create the role of Mélisande. Another triumph. As Massenet's Thaïs she inflamed her artistic success with her erotic enactment of the

1

courtesan—a performance which gave the public its stubborn opinion, however mistaken, about how "daring" her private life must be. For one year she was general manager of the great Chicago Opera, grandly bankrupting the company by the beauty and extravagance of her productions. James Gibbons Huneker and Carl Van Vechten had written paeans to her which I had read. Here was my chance to attend this great artist, and also take my mind off my trouble for a good part of the afternoon.

But it would help to be with friends. One came happily to mind—Natalie Hall, the operatic soprano. She and her mezzo-soprano sister Bettina were known for starring in a long-running Broadway operetta. I telephoned Natalie. To hear, to see Garden? Wildly grateful. Could she bring Bettina, whom I'd never met? We would meet, all three, at two forty-five in the Plaza Palm Court. I telephoned for reservations and was asked to take up the tickets by half past two—the ballroom was selling out. My day began to look up.

In good time I arrived at the Plaza, already somewhat insulated against my nervous state—but not for long. In the lobby was a portentous reminder—a large-lettered display announcing the day's events in the hotel:

MISS MARY GARDEN, LECTURE-RECITAL
3 P.M., Grand Ballroom
Second Floor South

And below that, ominously:

RECEPTION FOR MR. PAUL HORGAN
Harper & Brothers
5 to 7, White and Gold Suite
Second Floor North

There seemed to be no escape. At the box office I asked for my tickets. The young woman clerk shuffled them out and I was about to pay for them when behind her a tall, glossy, youngish man wearing a gardenia in his buttonhole snapped up the tickets, palmed my money aside, and said, "No, n'no, Mr. Horgan: with our compliments," and handed the three tickets to me.

"But why? Thank you, but I don't understand."

"I am Mr. Piza, Madame's manager. I have seen notice of your reception. My congratulations." Swarthy and elegant, he bowed like a South American. "We are delighted. Allow me."

Confused but elevated, I thanked him again and went to the Palm Court. There they were, the two beauties, one for each arm. Embraces. We made our way to the elevator.

"Garden: how exciting," said Natalie, the classic brunette, and Bettina, the glowing blonde, said, "Fabulous."

The ballroom was filling fast. We found our spindly gold chairs in a box on the right side of the room with a fine view of the small formal stage where a concert grand piano waited.

Suddenly the stage bloomed with light. There was a bated pause, and with a sudden step, Mary Garden appeared from stage right, halted, raised her arm to rest her hand on the proscenium, and held her pose. (A fleeting reminder of Toulouse-Lautrec's Yvette Guilbert.) Everyone stood. She let them, and then, with all standing, she made a wide gesture, showing the insides of her wrists, and leaned forward slowly in a bow that was not at all the grateful player's humble thanks, but a grant of permission to attend. She then went to the bend of the piano, poised in command, as the house settled. Already there was a sense of great occasion — how great, we did not then know, for it was her final appearance in public as a singer.

Small and delicate as she was, she had an affinity of countenance with the great cats, here refined exquisitely to retain the tiger's high cheeks above the fixed, meaningless smile; intent gaze; alert focus on all environs; thoughtless confidence of power; all supported by the gift of seeming beautiful at will. So, too, her movement, lithe, exact, gracile, was of the feline order. She was fifty-eight years old, she had abandoned the opera, and she was not any age. She was robed in who she was, which was enough to give the world.

Otherwise, her costume suggested both theater and salon, as best I can recall this — and all that follows.

She wore a close-fitting hat of black silk with a mesh of veil that came down just past her eyes — her eyes gleamed with a tigerish light in a little blue cave of shadow that put the years at a distance, and yet conveyed the vivid present. Her hair was a tawny gold. A floor-length fall of pale yellow satin, her gown was so tight over her straight hips that you wondered how she could step. A short-sleeved torero jacket in black sparkling stuff met long white gloves that reached above the elbows. A necklace of big pearls was looped once about her throat, with the rest of it swaying almost to her knees. How tall was she? A few inches over five feet, it was recorded somewhere; but she was a figure so commanding that illusion created height.

By her valiant posture she seemed to tell us not to be nervous — all would be well, indeed brilliant.

And it was.

She went right to work, saying something like, "Claude Debussy. The most fascinating yet mysterious public person I have ever met."

She then went on to speak for perhaps thirty minutes, in an international accent. Her tone was conversational, emphatic when proper, beguiling when memory was tender; always correct as to the language, though when she needed French, the pronunciation made no pretense to sound native.

In particles, then: Debussy was "a very strange man," as she wrote fifteen years later in her autobiography. (Much that she wrote and much that she said in her lecture are merged in my memory.) She said he was not tall, rather stocky. Quite extraordinarily, he had *two* foreheads — yes, two, one bulging on top over which he brushed his dark hair, the other showing in the clear above his black brows. His eyes, dark, sometimes quite expressionless, were fascinating. You never quite knew what he was thinking. Things he said were original, quite. He was mad about women, though one didn't know if he ever loved anyone, really. People always wondered, of course, some even asked, if he and she had ever been lovers. The idea was preposterous — not that he did not make the attempt one day on a railroad platform in Versailles, but no, there was nothing to it. A perfect artistic understanding, that was all, and it was enough. They rehearsed *Pelléas et Mélisande* for four months. Debussy attended, Messager conducted, they had forty orchestra rehearsals, unheard of. But when the opening came, Debussy was not there, and in fact he never attended a public performance. Some were offended. Not she. She understood when he said that for ten years the opera had been his life, and as he knew it best in that way, no other way was as real to him. When the role of Mélisande became hers at his desire, the author of the play, Maeterlinck, made a scandal, tried to have her removed in favor of his mistress, Mme Georgette Leblanc, but no, Debussy held fast, he never gave in, Mélisande remained hers, then, and for as long as she, and *she herself*, chose, in whatever opera company she was singing. Debussy had a devoted first wife, Lily, who adored him; she overlooked much, but never expected what happened, when he left her quite abruptly for a rich woman. Lily tried to kill herself, and at that he seemed concerned, but in the hospital when she assured him that she would now live, he shrugged and simply went away, and that was all of that. A very strange man, but yes, fascinating, a great pianist, though a poor singer when he sang the part to everyone in a first reading—his voice was small and husky. He adored Mélisande's voice (he always used that name instead of "Mary Garden") and he loved her voice so much that he composed and dedicated to her a whole group of songs, the *Ariettes*. . . .

And I remembered this when years afterward I read in his letters that Debussy wrote of her: "Le succès de 'notre Garden' ne m'étonne pas; il faudrait autrement avoir des oreilles bouchées à l'émeri pour résister au charme de sa voix. Pour ma part, je ne puis concevoir un timbre plus doucement insinuant. Cela ressemble même à de la tyrannie, tant il est impossible de l'oublier." (I am not amazed at the success of "our Garden"; you'd have to have your ears plugged by a ground-glass stopper to resist the spell of her voice. I can't imagine a timbre more softly persuasive. It's like a tyranny, impossible to put out of mind.)

And she remembered what he said of her to Carré, the director of the Opéra Comique, at a rehearsal of *Pelléas et Mélisande* while she was creating the character: *Je n'ai rien à lui dire*—he could suggest nothing to enhance her realization of the role. But that was how it always was with her work—she never *studied* how to do a part—she always simply *knew*, it came from nowhere, and it was always the truth. At the end of that particular rehearsal she heard him say to Carré, "What a strange person, this child." Then in his baffling, remote way, he picked up his hat and walked off—he was always doing that, suddenly walking out. . . .

In the Plaza Hotel Grand Ballroom, she was up to her old tricks—casting a spell, as she had done in countless opera performances. With her random notes on Claude Debussy, she brought him before us and we believed. When she finished speaking, she allowed a long thoughtful pause; and then, with peremptory grace, she turned toward the wings, extending her hand to bring forth her accompanist, Jean Dansereau, and a self-effacing youth who would turn pages. Now they would give us songs by Debussy, fourteen of them, including, according to the next day's *Times*, the air of *Lia* from *L'Enfant prodigue*, the third of the *Ariettes*, *Je tremble en voyant ton image*, *Green*, *La Chevelure*, and *Mandoline*. M. Dansereau, a small, wiry Frenchman, played the piano texts with a tonal intelligence equal to hers—by turns scintillant, brooding, declamatory.

How to be exact in describing a performance made of sound, that medium as fugitive as time? Her voice was without luster—she was past the age of brilliant tone. Perfect in pitch, it had at moments almost a *parlando* quality, in a timbre reminiscent of dried leaves stirred by air. But what expression, now smoky with passion, again rueful for life's shadows! What musicality; and what sense of meaning—the texts of Guignand, Bourget, Pierre Louÿs, Verlaine, Baudelaire came forth in all the beauty and power of Debussy's description: "the spell of her voice . . . so softly persuasive." We were persuaded. Did any artist more fully know who, and what, she was? Was this the first attribute of the interpretive genius?

For two hours I forgot my coming trial, and when the concert ended, my companions and I were in lingering thrall. I said we must try to go back-stage to pay our respects, and as singers, the Misses Hall agreed with stars in their eyes.

At the hidden entrance to the stage, then, I presented us to Mr. Piza, who was on guard there. Could we say one word to Miss Garden of our perfect fulfillment?

"Ah, thank you, I'm afraid not. You see, Madame never receives after a performance. But I will tell her. Thank you."

"No, it is our thanks," I said. And then, in a leap beyond the bounds of the plausible, I added, "But you so kindly invited me to your occasion, per-haps you would let me invite Madame and yourself to my own party," and I mentioned the reception for my new book, already under way at well after five.

"Yes, I know, of course. But again—" Mr. Piza was extremely polite in excusing Madame from unscheduled and, in fact, unexamined events.

We sighed and turned away. I began to feel the familiar stress under my necktie again. Natalie looked at me and said, "You'll be all right."

By her concern she drove home my dread. I nodded. Compelled to a brave show, I took the sisters to the lobby where I bought flowers for us all—violets for them to hold, a dark red carnation for my buttonhole.

"Let's go up, then," I said, viewing the elevator with its brass lace as a tumbril. But the Hall sisters had to leave me: they must have an early supper to be ready for their evening show. With a gaunt smile I embraced them and saw them go; and then I ascended to the White and Gold Suite on the second floor, to be discharged upon a waste of polished parquet. Three lofty rooms facing the park were thrown into one, which at first glance seemed almost empty.

Where was the party, that clamorous huddle of people at cocktails, shouting each other down with a high decibel count thermally stimulated by their massed body heat? But as I looked about I saw that there were guests present — perhaps sixty or so — who were ranged tightly on little gold chairs lining the walls. A few were talking to others beside them, others sat silent, holding drinks. In the center of the floor was a Harper group of three persons, waiting for me impassively. I advanced upon Mr. Cass Canfield, the publisher, Mr. Eugene Saxton, my first great editor, and Miss Ramona Herdman, the charming publicity chief.

"You're late," said Mr. Canfield dryly.

"Not fatally," said Mr. Saxton with his perpetually amused smile.

The wallside chairs became aware and glanced in my direction, but no moves were made. The party seemed enclosed in ice. A waiter came our way and I acquired a martini.

Finally, "Shouldn't you meet people?" asked Miss Herdman.

She took me to the wall and walked me along to shake hands as we went. The guests looked briefly at me and returned to their self-absorptions. I had a sense that every known Van Doren was present, and I recognized other glittering names, for none of which, of course, was mine a match. The gathering, meant to be festive, was lost to the lifeless inane. Something had to be done if Harper and Brothers were not to endure a total waste. The case was so poor — a young writer from the far provinces facing his first New York public event — that nothing was at risk, even to my making a fool of myself. If nobody would talk to me, I would invade them in another persona. To play the host, I became a waiter. I took a tray of canapés and began to go down the rows of gilt chairs offering a bite here, another there, which were accepted as intrusions or declined as interruptions.

And then: there should have been a fanfare for tympani and cymbals. Glancing along the wall in my duty I had a sudden shock of peripheral vision which made me turn sharply for a direct view.

There in the central doorway of the party rooms stood Mary Garden, in her pose of permitting herself to the public. As there was no one to announce her, she was waiting to be received. Behind her were the members of her *cuadrilla*, extending the symbol of her torero jacket: Mr. Piza; M. Jean Dansereau; the female secretary, Miss Croucher (or some such name) in tweeds; a maid holding two fur coats and three large handbags; and, hugging his music briefcase, the remote young man who turned pages. The great world was there for me.

I managed to set my tray down on a vacant chair and go to the doorway. Euphoria gave me character. Reaching the presence, I bowed like a Renaissance courtier and declared, I think ringingly, "Madame! You pay us an enchanting honor!"

With a piercing gleam out of her veiled cave, Mary Garden raised her right hand in a torchlike gesture and briskly demanded of her manager behind her shoulder, "Piza-who-is-this?"

"It is your host, Madame, Mr. Paul Horgan, for whom the reception is held."

"So it is. *Allons*."

And so it was that I led her procession into the room, while all around us the murmur arose, *Look, look, it's Mary Garden!* which she acknowledged only by a slight lift of her shoulders. I heard Mr. Canfield inquire flatly, "Was she invited?" and Miss Herdman reply, "No, I made the list," and I, feeling like someone else, said, "*I* invited her" and escorted Madame to the precise middle of the room, where in her habit of center stage she elected to take up her position. The *cuadrilla* ranged itself behind her. The gilt chairs were emptying fast as guests came about us to form a dense circle, though instinctively at a respectful distance. I was aloft in the translation of character which came to my rescue. As Harper and Brothers loomed a little nearer, politeness required that I say:

"Madame, may I introduce —"

"No-no," she interrupted in an elevated voice, "I will speak only to you," adding a smile worthy of Thaïs. An audience-hush fell over the company. There I was, trapped with glory and fame. What could I, must I, say further?

"May I offer you a drink, Madame?"

She excused the banality with a crosswise wave of her forefinger.

"A cigarette?"

"*Jamais — ma voix*."

With the genius of desperation I knew I must play above my form. I said, "This has been an historic afternoon for the centuries, Miss Garden!"

"You attended my *séance musicale*?"

"Yes, Madame, the event of a lifetime of musical events."

"Lifetime?" She made a smile of devastating wistfulness. "A lifetime: how old are you?"

"Thirty-two. But —"

"How perfect — neither an ending nor a beginning! But my afternoon —"

"Yes, the superb lecture. You hardly seemed to speak, Madame. You created pictures in the air."

"Pictures in the air. How lovely."

"Your text was astonishing. You spoke, not in phrases, not in sentences, but in paragraphs!"

"I did?" She commanded the *cuadrilla*. "Piza? Did you hear? Miss Croucher, write that down, make a note, so valuable, we must keep this."

She knew I was talking nonsense, but she felt the extremity that compelled it, and together we wrote our scene out of thin air in the ping-pong of drawing-room comedy.

"Yes," I said, "and the songs: never such musical line, never such penetration beyond what the poet meant!"

"Yes," she said, "poetry alone has never touched me, except to make me restless and nervous."

"Yes, good poetry is all nerves. When poetry is bracing, it is all bad."

"But then Debussy's music was always the right music for the words. Think of it: until we parted, but not as friends, he always said he was going to write an opera of Romeo and Juliet for me."

She spoke fast and imperiously, her voice a little edgy; and she made little steps in place, a miniature dance, to animate the scene and hold attention. Juliet invoked hazy romance. She measured me down and up with her veiled rays. I was only an underweight specimen at best, but . . .

"Piza, look at him!" she declaimed. "Did you ever see a figure more *soigné*?" She danced a little near me and reached out her white-gloved hands and molded my flanks, waist, and hips, and cried, "Don't, you must promise me, don't you ever gain a single pound!"

From the always-growing throng of onlookers came a wordless murmur that meant, *Really!*

"Tell me," she said, "what do you write? I hope novels. I adore novels. When I want the truth I go to fiction."

"Yes, a novel, *No Quarter Given*."

"No quarter: I never gave quarter. What is it about?"

"It's enormous. It's about —"

"What a novel I could write! Perhaps one day I shall. Though perhaps I have already lived my novel. One should never repeat. I shall never forget what someone said to me — was it Paul Bourget or Jacques-Emile Blanche?

I forget — one should never repeat except in love. You will write many more books. I must have them all, I am an excellent critic."

And so on, and so on, as the minutes flew. Questions like sparks that died away, with hardly a pause for an answer; and *le tout New York* craned and stared for every word and gesture. I did what I could to keep the ball in the air, and I broke the law only twice — once when my sister Rosemary (to whom my novel was dedicated) arrived, and I introduced her to Madame. Again, when I saw an old friend appear despite a state of mourning for her husband's recent death — Mrs. Isabel Ames of New Mexico. I was touched that under the circumstances she came to my party and I broke ranks to go to greet her. In the piercing voice of an elderly lady used to coping with deafness in the family, Mrs. Ames said:

"They tell me that you are talking to someone named Mary Garden. Is she anything to the real one?"

"It *is* the real one," I murmured, trying to hush my friend.

"My God," cried Mrs. Ames, a lifetime of laughter in her endearing old face, "I thought she was dead years ago!"

Madame's management of this cheerful affront was masterly. Everyone had heard it. All leaned to see what she would do about it. She simply grew tall, raised her gaze well above everyone present, and defied comment. The effect of vitality was immense. In an instant I was back in her service. Finger on lip, she brooded a moment, and then:

"I want to ask you something — you *will* do it, won't you: I want you to do it: you are the one to do it: I can tell, I can *always* tell, you are the one to do it."

"But anything, Miss Garden, of course."

"Then I want you to write a play for me — a delicious three-act comedy of manners, very high style, *gaie comme les hirondelles*, witty, blazing with epigrams, don't you know, yet with an undertone of sadness — not *sad*, don't you know, but *triste*, like a lovely day in autumn and full of love — *amusing* love, don't you know, nobody throwing themselves about, but so touching. And please: Mr. Horgan: give me just one little song to sing? the second act? perhaps, yes, I think, just before the curtain, so the *meaning* of the song will come to us in the *last* act! Do you think?"

With becoming extravagance I agreed to write the play. A book news reporter or two made notes. Mr. Canfield loomed open-mouthed. Mr. Saxton beamed indulgently. The comedy was running down. Mr. Piza leaned across Madame's shoulder and showed her his watch, made murmur about waiting obligations; and, facing me — "Ah!" — the white-gloved hand rose to the brow deploring the second-rate demands made upon the numinous.

"I must go. Send me your novel, Hotel Pierre. I will read it. I will write you instantly about it. You have been gallant. We must meet soon again. Do not neglect my play."

She made a sweeping turn toward the exit, creating a parabola of knee-length pearls, and I escorted her away with the *cuadrilla* in tow. As I bent to kiss her hand, I caught a glimpse of the smile with which she made an open secret of the farce in our scene; and then she dutifully held a farewell pose in the elevator gates. The gates clanged shut. Behind me, the crowd had shifted to observe insatiably, someone started to clap, the ovation grew, and to farewell applause, Mary Garden's car descended with the effect of a great sigh of release.

I returned to the party. It was exploding in a clamor of talk. Everyone had the same thing to talk about. The ice was not only broken, it was shattered. I was besieged with questions — what else had she said; did she mean it all; had I known her before; where; would I really write her a play; tell about your novel; do you often come East from New Mexico. Suddenly, in the New York way, I had many ten-minute friends. Briefly I was a hero. Nobody left before nine o'clock.

On the following morning I went to Brentano's where I inscribed a copy of *No Quarter Given* to Mary Garden and asked that it be sent to her at the Pierre Hotel. In hopes of a rapturous reply, I included my hotel address. Nothing came from her, about either the novel or our future collaboration. After some days of growing realism, I telephoned the Pierre Hotel. Miss Garden had checked out days ago.

Any forwarding address?

"Of course not," replied the Pierre Hotel coldly, in defense of the vanishing point of celebrity.

Edmund Wilson at Oxford

I met Edmund Wilson, I think, sometime in the early spring of 1946, after I had come back from Moscow to finish the job I was doing at the British Embassy in Washington. I had been in Washington during the war years, and my friend the Russian composer Nicolas Nabokov, who, like his cousin Vladimir, was a friend of Wilson's, thought that he might like to meet me (I had expressed my intense admiration for *Axel's Castle* and *The Triple Thinkers*) and talk about Russian literature and other topics. Wilson refused. He was convinced that any British official could only want to meet him in order to rope him into the British propaganda machine. He was acutely isolationist: his Anglophobia, which in any case had been fairly acute, was increased by the reflection that England had once again managed to drag America into a dreadful and totally unnecessary war, and he had no wish to meet any representative of that country. However, once the war was over he evidently decided that he was no longer in any danger of being inveigled into pro-British activities, and asked me to lunch at the Princeton Club in New York.

I was, I own, taken aback by his appearance. I do not know what I had imagined a distinguished literary critic to look like, but there stood before me a thickset, red-faced, potbellied figure, not unlike President Hoover in appearance; but once he began to talk, almost before we had sat down, I forgot everything save his conversation. He spoke in a curiously strangled voice, with gaps between his sentences, as if ideas jostled and thrashed about inside him, getting in each other's way as they struggled to emerge, which made for short bursts, emitted staccato, interspersed with gentle, low-voiced, legato passages. He spoke in a moving and imaginative fashion about the American writers of his generation, about Dante, and about what the Russian poet Pushkin had meant to him. He described his visit to the Soviet Union in (I think) the middle thirties and the appalling effect which this had had upon him, for, like many other members of the American intelligentsia, he had once tended to idealize the Communist regime. The climax of his visit was a meeting with Prince D. S. Mirsky. Mirsky was a brilliant, highly original émigré writer in English on Russian literature who had become a convert to Marxism in England; he then returned to Russia and soon after this published a book denouncing British writers and intellectuals, some of whom had befriended him. Wilson found him in Moscow in a very low and wretched state (a few years later he was arrested and sent to a camp and liquidated). Mirsky's downfall and pathetic condition had made an indelible impression on Wilson, and he spoke long and bitterly about the passing of his own political infatuation. He then talked about Russian literature in general, and particularly about Chekhov and Gogol, as well as I have ever heard anyone talk on any literary topic. I was completely fascinated; I felt honored to have met this greatly gifted and morally impressive man. We became friends. I did not return to the United States until 1949, when I went to teach at Harvard, and stayed a night with Wilson at Wellfleet, where he was living with his wife Elena. I went to see them both on subsequent visits in the fifties.

In 1954 he came to England and telephoned virtually from the airport to tell me that he wished to come to Oxford and stay with me for a day or two. I welcomed this. Since I was not married then, I was living in All Souls College. Wilson did indeed stay two nights with me in a not very attractive college room (which I think he describes with characteristic acerbity in one of his letters). He was in a splendidly Anglophobic mood. On the first morning, before lunch, we went for a walk to look at the colleges. When we passed through Christ Church, he looked at the decaying building of the Library (not then yet refaced, as it would be later, with the assistance of the Rockefeller Foundation) and said, "Oh, most of these buildings look in very poor shape — I think they're actually falling down," and looked delighted. "I think that's the case with a lot of England," he went on, "I think your country deserves a bit of this."

He then launched into a sweeping attack on academic life and academics in general as murderers of all that was living and real in literature and art — classical, medieval, modern. I asked him whether there were no academics he liked or admired. He said that there were indeed a few: one was Christian Gauss, his teacher at Princeton, whose lectures he had greatly admired and whom he had liked and deeply respected as a man; another was Norman Kemp Smith, who had been a professor of philosophy at Prince-

ton in his day and was now living in retirement in Scotland. (Wilson had
gone to see him during a visit to England in 1945, the visit on which the
pages about England in *Europe without Baedeker* were founded.) Apart
from these he could, for the moment, think of no one.

The diatribe continued (I had no idea of whether this was a passing
mood, induced by Oxford, or a permanent attitude): He could wish for no
worse fate for anyone than to hold a job at a university, particularly if it
were connected with literary studies; he had heard that Archibald
MacLeish contemplated becoming, or had become, a professor somewhere,
was it Harvard? It was a fate that that ass deserved (I had read Wilson's
devastating parody, "The Omelet of A. MacLeish," and had realized that
this poet was not one of his favorites). Then there had been the ridiculous
Ted Spencer at Harvard, who tried to seek him out but had died before any
relationship could be attempted; and there was also Spencer's protégé,
Harry Levin — a clever man, and widely read, with interesting things to say,
who had had it in him to become something if only he had not chosen to
make a career at Harvard, which had turned him into a pedantic school-
master, buried in trivial detail, dryasdust, who turned everything into dust,
a kind of colored dust. "Oh, but I can't explain it," he said, "I talked to him
about Howells — he doesn't think Howells is any good at all." He went on
to say that Harry Levin was, in spite of all this, not a bad fellow; he could
be highly perceptive and interesting, but he was ridiculous about Howells.
I was under the impression that they were friends (as I feel sure in fact they
were) and was taken aback by these remarks about Levin, whom I admired
and whose essay on Stendhal I thought a remarkable piece of work. But
he would not relent. His next target was Perry Miller; then C. S. Lewis; he
went on and on in a ferocious fashion. Perhaps Tennyson talked about
Churton Collins in this way when he called him a louse in the locks of literature. I saw no reason to doubt that he spoke of me in similar fashion; it
was obviously part of him; I loved him as he was.

He asked me whether it was to be his fate to meet more academics at
lunch or dinner. I relieved his fears about lunch by saying the guests would
be Stephen Spender and another man of letters (I cannot remember who);
in the evening, however, if he wished to dine in All Souls as he had suggested, he might well meet some academics. Would he prefer to dine in a
restaurant? No, he said, he wished to plumb the depths of old, decayed,
conservative English academic life in its death throes — I remember his

words: "It can't be long now," he said ominously, "I think we're in at the kill." I did not ask him to develop this theme, but tried to divert him onto other subjects. No good. He said that in England—London—writers and the like formed little cliques, jealous coteries engaged in keeping each other out; there was no real literary world; Evelyn Waugh could not be in a room with Peter Quennell, a perfectly decent man of letters; both had spoken ill of Cyril Connolly; Auden was ostracized; nobody had a kind word to say about MacNeice or Angus Wilson; and so on and so on. Most of this seemed absurdly misconceived to me. To get him off this topic I asked him—unwisely, as it turned out—what his last visit to England had been like. But by then it was time for lunch. He seemed to enjoy the company, denounced the writers of the *Partisan Review*, said that Philip Rahv was able enough but, like the rest of them, used literature to make political points, and praised V. S. Pritchett as one of the few critics whose thought was free and who had something to say.

After lunch he reminded me of my earlier question and told me what had occurred during his previous London visit. He had arrived as a kind of war correspondent, and the wartime British Ministry of Information had detached the well-known publisher Hamish Hamilton, who was then a member of that ministry and was half American, to look after him. Hamilton had organized a party of eminent members of the British literary establishment. According to Wilson, he saw at the party, among others, T. S. Eliot, one or two Sitwells, Cyril Connolly, Siegfried Sassoon, Harold Nicolson, Peter Quennell, and, I think, Rosamond Lehmann. He wished to talk to none of these. "T. S. Eliot," he said, "is a gifted poet, but somewhere inside him there is a scoundrel. When I see him, which is not often, I just cannot take him. I do not wish to meet him, although I think some of his poetry is wonderful—it repels me, but it is poetry." The Sitwells he dismissed as being of no interest. The only person there that he was able to speak to was Compton Mackenzie—they swapped stories about life before and during the First World War, and he found the appearance, manner, and conversation of the old buccaneer quite entrancing.

I gradually realized that there is a sense in which Wilson belonged to an earlier generation than the literary intelligentsia of England at that time; that the kind of people he preferred were the Edwardians—full-blooded, masculine men of letters, with sometimes coarse (and even to some degree philistine) but vital personalities—and that this was the world to which

Compton Mackenzie truly belonged. Desmond McCarthy had once described to David Cecil and myself a typical dinner he had attended some years before the First World War in a London club — the Reform, or it may have been the Travellers. Present were Rudyard Kipling, H. G. Wells, Max Beerbohm, Hilaire Belloc, G. K. Chesterton, Arnold Bennett, and Bernard Shaw, as well as Henry James and the young Hugh Walpole. There was no talk about literature or the arts, or friendship or nature or morality or personal relations or the ends of life — the kinds of things that were discussed in Bloomsbury. There was not a touch of anything faintly aesthetic — the talk was hearty, concerned with royalties, publishers, love affairs, absurd adventures, society scandals, and anecdotes about famous persons, accompanied by gusts of laughter, puns, limericks, a great deal of mutual banter, jokes about money, women, and foreigners, and with a great deal of drink. The atmosphere was that of a male dining club of vigorous, amusing, sometimes rather vulgar friends. These were the best-known authors of the time, the "blind leaders of the blind" so much disliked and disapproved of by Bloomsbury. It seemed to me that Edmund Wilson, for all his unerring sense of quality and his moral preoccupations, had an affinity with these masters. I do not think that he would have greatly enjoyed tea with Mrs. Woolf or an evening with Lytton Strachey.

Hence the literary party in London did not suit him at all, and, after a few perfunctory words with E. M. Forster about Jane Austen, he told Hamish Hamilton that he wanted to get away from it as soon as possible. After the conversation with Compton Mackenzie he swiftly withdrew, to the disappointment, so Hamilton told me, of some of those invited. All he wished to do was to go to Scotland and see his mentor, Kemp Smith. Hamish Hamilton, who had probably never heard of this Kantian scholar, did his best to arrange for the journey to Scotland. Wilson did manage to see him — he told me that he had had a good time with him, that they had talked about the old times with great pleasure and had discussed the decline in the standards of European scholarship. Then he came back to London to be met at the station by the courteous and indefatigable Hamilton, who tried to persuade him to get into a taxi to go to his hotel. It was evening; Wilson had become convinced (so he told me) that what Hamilton was mainly anxious to do was to prevent him from seeing the prostitutes who then walked the streets of London in exceptional numbers (so he had been told). He did his best to evade Hamilton, for whom he had by then conceived one of his violent, irrational dislikes (by this time reciprocated by Hamilton, who told me on a later occasion that Wilson was one of the most unpleasant and difficult people he had ever encountered). Wilson did get into a taxi, but, by God, he got out of it after five minutes, and he *did* walk the streets, particularly Park Lane, and he *did* see prostitutes, and he felt that he had scored off the officials who had been sent to escort him, almost, he thought, in the manner of the Russian secret police.

I tried to persuade him that all that Hamish Hamilton had attempted to do was to extend the kind of courtesies which cultural institutions thought to be his due. Wilson would have none of that: he was certain that an attempt was being made to bear-lead him in London, to prevent him from meeting unsuitable people whom in fact he might have liked to meet. This conviction — that there was a general conspiracy in England, of a Soviet type, not to let him meet unsuitable people — obsessed him, and was to surface later in Oxford. I asked him if he had disliked every literary person he had met in London. He said, "No, I liked Evelyn Waugh and Cyril Connolly best." Why? "Because I thought they were so nasty." Perhaps this referred to later meetings, because I do not know if Evelyn Waugh was in London during the war in which he served as a soldier. He had also taken to Angus Wilson because he reminded him of the heartfelt human feelings of the kind of Americans with whom he felt at home. It was the aestheticism, the prissiness, the superciliousness, the cliquishness, the thin, piping voices, the bloodlessness, the preoccupation with one's own emotions both in life and in literature — all of which he (no less than D. H. Lawrence) attributed to Bloomsbury — that irritated him. He thought the whole of English literary life was infected by this. I don't know what he would have said about J. B. Priestley — I think that he was, perhaps, below his angle of vision. He could not bear the thought of the Huxleys, Aldous or Julian.

Evening fell, and it was time for dinner in the Common Room of All Souls College. He had me on one side and the senior Fellow dining, the historian A. L. Rowse, on the other. He hardly spoke to Rowse, although Rowse tried to speak to him. He turned to me brusquely and engaged in conversation about mutual friends in America — Justice Felix Frankfurter and his wife, Nicolas Nabokov and his wives, the playwright Sam Behrman, Mary McCarthy (to whom Wilson had been married), Conrad Aiken, Arthur Schlesinger, Judge Learned Hand, and others. Reluctantly he turned to his other side and allowed himself to be addressed by Rowse. He answered in monosyllables. After coffee, when we came back to my rooms, he complained that a flood of British nationalist propaganda had been poured over him by Rowse at dinner, that he had not come to Oxford to be made a victim of cultural chauvinists. I think that on a later occasion, when Rowse went to see him in the United States, they may have got on a little better — but on this occasion he was in a grumpy mood and would not let up.

He said that he realized why the All Souls College servants removed the plates so rapidly, hardly letting him finish a single dish — he spoke of a Barmecide feast — it was because they were acutely class-conscious, hated their masters, wanted to serve them as gracelessly as possible, and get away from their hated presence as quickly as they could. He had noticed, he said, that class consciousness was clearly rampant in this ancient establishment. I did not argue with him — he was, I think, past convincing on this and most other points. What he said was characteristic wonderful nonsense, of course. The majority of scouts (servants) in Oxford were certainly then, and perhaps are still, among the most conservative of its inhabitants; they were conscious carriers of ancient College traditions, old retainers if ever there were such, who for the most part — certainly at that time — refused to be unionized on the ground that this was an insult to what they conceived to be their status and very special function. The servants at All Souls exemplified this type almost to the point of caricature.

It was plain that Wilson on that day — as on many others — lived in a world of angry fantasy, particularly in the case of anything British, and although I was devoted to him, felt deep admiration and respect for him to his dying day, and remain intensely proud of the friendship that bound us, I knew that it was useless to argue with him once he got the bit between his teeth. This was certainly the case during his stay with me in Oxford. After dinner I had invited my colleague David Cecil, the novelist Iris Murdoch and her husband the critic John Bayley, and the philosopher Stuart Hampshire to meet him. It was not a happy evening. He took against everyone in the room. He mistook Bayley for the critic Humphry House (with whom he might well have got on) and virtually ignored him and everyone else. He became listless, answered in monosyllables, gurgled, drank a great deal of whiskey, and looked with hateful eyes at everyone. Although Iris, who is the soul of courtesy and kindness, tried to make things go, and John Bayley, a beguiling talker, did his best, the old bear remained in his lair, glaring balefully from time to time and trying to drown his boredom in drink. The evening came to an early end. At the end of it he burst out about these feeble creatures — aristocrats who dabbled in literature were useless; the dons were all bloodless monks, cut off from all that mattered. Why could I not have invited one of the few academics with guts, like A. J. P. Taylor, whom he wanted to meet because he liked his radical polemics? I said that I knew and liked Taylor, despite a slight *froideur* caused by a somewhat disparaging review he had written of a small book I had just published, but that I would gladly arrange a meeting between them — and did so on the following day.

Taylor was most amiable to us both. Wilson said that he had quite enjoyed his visit to Taylor's rooms in Magdalen College. But then Taylor had taken him to a lecture by Steven Runciman on a Byzantine subject, which bored him stiff; once again he heard the over-refined and, to him, deeply depressing accents of Bloomsbury, those high, thin voices which he could not bear. (I do not know how many of these voices he had ever actually heard.) I also arranged for him to see the Jewish historian Cecil Roth, because at this time he took an increasing interest in Jewish history and was learning Hebrew — it was not long before his book on the Dead Sea Scrolls. That visit also went well, particularly as I had warned him that Roth was something of a bore, though a worthy and learned antiquary; those mildly disparaging words were enough to make Wilson like him. He muttered something about being kept from people he admired by persons (myself) who for some reason decided to "blackball" them — more fantasy, more mild paranoia. Once he had formed a sociological and psychological hypothesis, he held onto it grimly with a kind of pleased, deliberate perversity, against all evidence. He told me that the only persons he had truly enjoyed meeting in England, apart from his old friend Sylvester Gates, whom he had known at Harvard many years before, were Connolly (again, because what he said was so malicious), Taylor, Roth, and Angus Wilson. The rest seemed to him repellent. "And Compton Mackenzie? And Kemp Smith?" Yes, indeed, these too, but that was all. The most hateful figure to him in England, he said, was Winston Churchill, who was nothing but a typical low-grade American journalist. If it were not for Sylvester Gates and myself he would not have come to England. Did Oxford still contain a ridiculous puffed-up fellow called Maurice Bowra, whom he had met with Gates and who, for all his knowledge of languages, had no understanding whatever of literature? He loved literature — that was evident — a pity that he had nothing of interest to say about it; he gathered that he was a friend of mine: how could this be? His conversation was banal and empty to a degree, just a lot of shouting. He could not understand how such writers as Cyril Connolly and Evelyn Waugh could be said to owe so much to this inflated philistine — they were at least gifted, he was a caricature John Bull. The diatribes went on. By this time he had drunk a great deal and his eyes were almost closed. I managed to get him to his bedroom, not without some difficulty.

Next day he was serene and gentle. We talked about Russian writers, about his life in Talcottville, which he pressed me to visit with him, about Hebrew tenses and the structure of the Hungarian language (which he contemplated acquiring), about his intense admiration for the poetry of W. H. Auden, about the interesting position of the *New Yorker* in American cultural life, about the monstrously patronizing attitude of Europeans, not only the despicable English but the French and even the Italians, toward American culture, toward such great poets as Walt Whitman and such prose writers as Herman Melville and Henry James — they were recognized, but the fact that they were Americans had always, it seemed to him, to be explained away or apologized for. But America would show them. There was a wonderful generation of young technologists and engineers coming up in America, confident, gifted, clearheaded, uncluttered men in thin drill suits (I remember this odd description), inventors of excellent new gadgets; these men were building a new, fresh, highly practical civilization that would respond to new human needs and would open prospects of wonderful new comforts of life, and this would supersede the decay and self-conceit and squalor of a fast-declining, petty-minded European culture. Nevertheless, these *boutades* of his were less violent than on the day before, and rarer. Wilson was in a calmer and happier mood, quite relaxed. He explained that his life was, and always had been, literature and writers, that music* and even painting meant less, even though they did mean a great deal: Malraux was marvelous on sculpture. Nothing had contributed so much to his ideas about life and art — to what seemed to him to matter, politics and all — as the great Russian masters. Pushkin had begun to move

---

* I once asked him, I cannot think why, whether he liked Wagner. He said, I think, "Yes, yes, I did, yes, when I was much younger, but it is not the kind of stuff I can listen to now."

him more than Shakespeare, but not more than Dante; what terrible nonsense Orwell had written about Tolstoy and Lear. He said that his distaste
for the English had been increased by the knock-kneed creatures he met
in London and Oxford. Did I know his friend Jason Epstein? He was, he
thought, himself misanthropic enough, but Epstein outdid him — his dislike
of mankind was phenomenal. He liked Epstein, and liked that in him.

After which he left. It could not be regarded as a successful visit. In spite
of this, he did come back to Oxford with his wife Elena to stay for a couple
of days with me and my wife — by that time we were living in a house of
our own — and I took care not to invite Oxford academics to meet him,
however great their eagerness and admiration. I preferred to meet him in
Boston, London, and New York.

He is, in my eyes, a great critic, and a noble and moving human being,
whom I loved and respected and wanted to have a good opinion of me; I
was deeply touched when, not long before he died, he made me inscribe
a line from the Bible with a diamond upon the windowpane of his house
in Wellfleet, a privilege reserved for friends. The line was a verse from
Isaiah, with whom, he insisted, I had obviously identified myself — another
ineradicable fantasy, like his obstinate insistence that I had only written as
I did about Tolstoy because I, too, was a fox, longing to be, indeed believing
myself to be, a hedgehog. Nothing said to deny this absurdity made the
faintest impression on him. He knew that "like all Jews," I sought unity and
a metaphysical integrated organic world; in fact, I believe the exact opposite. The constructions of his inner world withstood all external evidence.
He was prey to wild fantasies, to absurd conjectures, to irrational hatreds
and loves. The fact that my prejudices largely coincided with his own was,
of course, an immense source of sympathy and endearment. It was perhaps
this more than anything else that brought us together.

His judgments were often erratic, and he was prey to delusions, but his
humanity and integrity were total. When he went off on a tangent it might
end anywhere. His review in the *New Yorker* of Pasternak's *Doctor Zhivago*
was the best and most understanding, I think, in any language; but his
speculation in a later article on the meaning of various names and symbols
in the novel was crazy to a degree. He managed to combine profound
insight and extraordinary vision into cultures not his own with turbulent
prejudices, hatreds, and a great deal of pure nonsense; he sometimes
misfired totally and missed the target by miles; yet most of his denuncia-

tions were deserved. He was the last major critic in the tradition of Johnson, Sainte-Beuve, Belinsky, and Matthew Arnold; his aim and practice were to consider works of literature within a larger social and cultural frame — one which included an absorbed, acutely penetrating, direct, wonderfully illuminating view of the author's personality, goals, and social and personal origins, the surrounding moral, intellectual, and political worlds, and the nature of the author's vision — and to present the writer, the work, and its complex setting as interrelated, integrated wholes. He told me during his visit that the modern tendency toward purely literary scholarship, toward an often deliberate ignoring of the texture of the writer's life and society, for him lacked all genuine content. I agreed with him, fervently. Art shone for him, but not by its own light alone. He is gone, and has not left his peer.

JULIAN BARNES

Playing Chess with Arthur Koestler

GAME 1

We play not on a board but on a curious rubber traveling mat. Perhaps it was originally magnetized to make the pieces hold firmly to their squares, but if so, the magnetism has long worn off. The mat has been rolled up for many years and does not flatten out properly, despite Arthur's smoothings. The surface dips and sways like undulating meadowland: bishops look even more threatening as they cant toward you at twenty degrees to the perpendicular. Those who play chess know how in the course of a game that bland grid of sixty-four squares becomes charged with lines of energy, pockets of power, backwoods domains of stagnancy and despair. As the isobars of control and vulnerability develop, this ruckled mat throws in some extra uncertainties, some distracting bits of dream and surrealism.

We begin cautiously: neither of us has played for some time. Every so often I am interrupted by the thought, *I'm playing chess with Arthur Koestler!* While it's normal to imagine how your opponent is assessing your game (will he buy that bluff? does he know I prefer bishops to knights?), it's less helpful to start worrying about what your opponent will think of you off the board because of what you do on it. But these considerations are hard to put aside when playing someone you have long admired, whose work spoke with a personal clarity during your intellectually formative years — and someone, after all, who reported the Fischer-Spassky match in Reykjavík for the London *Observer*. What does such a man think as I swap knights to double a pawn on his KB file? Is he judging this a crude maneuver that achieves a petty, vulgar advantage when one ought to be aiming for elegance, beauty, and finesse? Or is he saying to himself — like any other

23

normal chess-playing human—"Oh damn, why did I let this whipper-snapper double my pawns like that?"

Our rustiness, the joke "board," and the normal half-ludic, half-social uncertainties of playing an unfamiliar opponent are compounded by Arthur's physical condition. He is now seventy-seven, and known to be suffering from Parkinson's disease. When I arrive he remarks, in front of his wife Cynthia, how much he has deteriorated in the last twelve months. "Zis Parkinson's—it knocks me sidevays," he says in that almost parodic Middle European accent which still comes as a surprise because you somehow expect mastery of written and spoken English to go together. (But of course they don't. See Nabokov: "I think like a genius, I write like a distinguished author, and I speak like a child.") Arthur's hand movements have lost their precision, and perhaps his eyesight is not so good anymore, because occasionally during our five games he starts to put a piece down on an impossible square, awarding himself, for example, two bishops on the same diagonal. Usually he notices; once or twice I have to point it out (and do not like to ask whether the fault is one of hand or eye). Each time, he apologizes courteously: "Zis Parkinson's, it knocks me sidevays."

The game is tedious and barely competent until I get a useful pawn pin. He struggles to shift it and loses another pawn, then I rack up the pin, he semi-blunders, and I win rook for bishop. This, I know, is the key breakthrough: queens are already off, and my two rooks look unstoppable. Then it's my turn to blunder. Like many average players, I have a visceral fear of the opponent's knight. Bishops, queens, and rooks move in that straight-forward, undeceitful way of theirs; the knight—well, the opponent's knight—is sneaky and treacherous. Predicting the piece's behavior more than two moves ahead is almost impossible. So suddenly, without any decent notice at all, Arthur's whinnying horse is right in where it shouldn't be, forking my rook and king. All that hard work wasted, I think. "Analyzing the position" (as we describe sitting there and worrying a lot), I see that when he takes my rook, I recapture the knight, and we're level on material again. A long, grim struggle to come. So I move my king and *bang*, his next move is not, as I expect, to take off my rook, but to contrive a very neat mate with two bishops and knight. Ouch. You do like to be allowed at least to foresee the manner of your impending defeat. Oh well. 1–0.

GAME 2

It's the summer of 1982, and I am down at the Koestlers' farmhouse in Denston, Suffolk, for a week. I seem to be writing two novels at the same time, one of which is about Flaubert. Writers divide into those who happily talk about their work in progress and those who squirm in embarrassment at the prospect. I am a squirmer (of course, it's not just embarrassment; it's also caution that someone might steal the idea for your book, plus sheer vanity — however good you make it sound you probably won't be able to convey the full originality, daring, and brilliance of the project). Three or four times over the last year or so Arthur has asked me what I am working on, and each time I answer, with tight-lipped paranoia, "A book about Flaubert." Each time — preferring, as is his style, the challenging question to the mollifying expression of interest — he responds, "Why not Maupassant?" I never really find an answer. I suppose I should just say "Flaubert's better."

I stay in the visitor's flat at the end of the farmhouse. I write in the morning, have lunch, read, play chess with Arthur, and go for a run in the early evening (I am in what I hopefully refer to as "training" for the London Marathon, which is a safe nine months away). The weather stays fair, and a satisfying balance is held between work, exercise, and pleasure. The only bogus thing about my day is the "training." I have decided to avoid an over-hasty buildup to the twenty-six miles, and so jog around the unfrequented Suffolk lanes for twenty minutes or so, each day making it to a slightly more distant tree, a different patch of cow parsley. All kinds of mental stratagems have to be employed (dreaming up dinners, playing through sexual fantasies) to keep my legs moving, to rebuff the tempting voice which says, "What are you doing this for, you don't need this running shit, nobody can see you, come on, give up. . . ." But I just about don't give up in my low-level quest for a certain healthiness.

Arthur, as it later turns out, is worse than he lets on: he has leukemia as well as Parkinson's. Both diseases are to some extent controllable, though one or the other will get him in the end. One example of his "deterioration," he says, is that his voice is no longer reliable. It tires quickly and he can't always control the register; recently he's been turning down requests for radio and television interviews, and won't do any more. I fail to notice any fluctuations in his voice over two and a half hours the first evening, so am only half-convinced of his supposed decline, but he knows better. As it transpires, he is already planning his suicide. He has always been a firm and public believer in what is — either euphemistically or accurately, I can never quite decide — referred to as "self-deliverance." EXIT, the British organization founded to promote the cause of euthanasia, has produced a booklet offering practical advice. Arthur, in his methodical way, has already annotated his copy with a précis of what to do: "1. An hour and a half before your meal. . . ." He summarizes the amounts of drink and drugs specified, and notes for future use the shelf life of barbiturates ("eight years").

The second game lasts longer than the first, about an hour and three-quarters. Playing white, I open with a fianchettoed bishop. There is occasionally some mild surprise value in this beginning, though I use it mainly because it tends to lead to open, attacking chess. I hate and fear those clogged games with a great ball of pawn tension in the middle of the board; one minor miscalculation and the whole thing will suddenly unravel in your face. I remind myself that Bent Larsen, the Danish grand master famous for his attacking style, frequently opens with a fianchettoed bishop. As I play p-QN3 followed by B-N2, I dream of a pair of bishops on neighboring diagonals aiming their crossbows into the heart of black's defensive nest. But it seems I am not as good a chess player as Bent Larsen. A lot of pins and semi-pins hinder the bold maneuvers I have imagined. My diagonal threats peter out. Another loss. 2–0.

GAME 3

After the second game, I mention to Arthur that I've never played the King's Gambit. Whenever I try it out by myself, it always seems to lead to a lost position for white: it is suicidal. I only know one person — a reckless, pressing daredevil on the board — who ever plays this sharp, aggressive, old-fashioned gambit. So I ought to be less surprised when Arthur, as white, opens p-K4, p-KB4. I think, *Oh shit, the King's Gambit! I should never have told him how unfamiliar I am with it.* I picture him sneaking off the previous evening to his chess manuals and running through all the subtleties of this violent opening. Such thoughts don't help black's defenses; also, the suicidal tendencies implicit for white whenever I rehearse the King's Gambit seem mystifyingly absent for my opponent.

Now, toward the very end of his life, Arthur is mellowed by weakness. In the three or four years I have known him, he has become much less combative. I met him first at his house in Montpelier Square, at one of those London dinners at which most of those present have two houses and yet (and therefore) spend a lot of time complaining about the trade unions. It seems *de rigueur* on these occasions to have in your wallet a cutting from the *Daily Telegraph* about some obscure restrictive practice whereby workers with metal-boring drills are bringing the country to its knees by refusing to use their drills for boring wood. I was working for the *New Statesman* at the time (and living in a bed-sitter), so was unsusceptible to the inference that if only these recalcitrant workers would allow themselves to be pushed around a bit more, then people with two houses could afford a third house (which conclusion has been well borne out as Mrs. Thatcher's Britain continues). There was much disgust and dismay expressed that evening about the behavior of the National Graphical Association – the printers then being the particular object of fashionable odium among right-thinking people. (Quite by chance, I had spent that day at a small printing works in Southend, supervising the going-to-press of the *Statesman*'s back half. Everyone there had been hardworking, cooperative, and entirely lacking in a forked tail.) Not long after Mrs. Thatcher became leader of the Conservative Party, she paid a visit to Arthur. A previous prime minister, Harold Wilson, had recruited two famous Hungarian economists, Balogh and Kaldor, to his staff of special advisors. Arthur recalled that he was flattered by Mrs. Thatcher's attention but declined her casting: "I will not be your Hungarian guru."

Now he sits in the sunshine, with Mozart on the radio and a bottle of Moselle in a wine cooler before him, looking rather like a wise squaw. He walks with a stick and seems weary of his reputation for belligerence. I have recently read a new biography of Camus, and mention – thinking it might amuse him – that the historical record is confused. Some authorities maintain that he gave Camus a black eye only once; others assert that it was twice. But he is not particularly amused. "Only once," he says wearily. "It was a drunken brawl."

Despite my trepidation when faced with the King's Gambit, I seem to have chances at first; then Arthur establishes a strong center. A potential weakness is that he leaves his queen and knight on the same diagonal. But how to exploit this without being obvious? Gratifyingly, the weakness exploits itself: a forced defensive pawn-push on my part sets up a square for my bishop, which leaps out from the back rank into a killer pin on knight and queen. The queen falls. Some peril remains, as Arthur has two attacking rooks, two bishops, and a knight, plus a pawn on the sixth rank, but once all chances of a breakthrough are headed off he gently topples his king. 2–1.

Afterwards, I go for a run, light-headed and light-hearted. *Hey, I've beaten Arthur Koestler at chess!* There is nobody, alas, to tell; but I run for twenty-eight minutes nonstop, the longest for ages, without feeling too bad. When my calves begin to ache, I imagine lush country wives with throbbing décolletages who drive up alongside and implore me to take a lift; then I don't think of my calves for a while. But reality being what it is, there are no beckoning *chauffeuses*; I seem to have chosen a road driven only by careless and surly males.

GAME 4

While we are on the subject of literary brawls, there's something else to clear up. That famous occasion Arthur threw a bottle at Sartre, was it the same brawl as when he gave Camus a black eye, or a separate one? "I *never* threw a bottle at Sartre," he replies. The record on that, he insists, is false. He adds that his friendship with Sartre was "poisoned" by "Simone."

I open p-QB4, which Arthur says he has never played against (can this be true? well, it will be in this sense, that my first few moves are always divertingly ungrounded in opening theory). After a tense beginning, Arthur gradually puts on the K-side pressure and establishes — revenge for the last game — an unbreakable pin on knight and queen. For a while, I am forced into a mixture of last-ditch defense and a series of waiting moves (never good for morale). Then I see the chance of a possible breakthrough: I give up the pinned knight for two central pawns, which opens routes to his isolated king which he has overconfidently neglected to castle. Gradually, I increase the pressure and cram him into back-row submission. After an hour and a half of unremitting tension, I pummel my way to victory. 2–2.

With the game over, Arthur puts the pieces back on the board and dismisses one of his moves as a blunder — or rather, given his joke-shop pronunciation, "a blonder." If I hadn't mated him, he points out, he would have mated me. So far we have played four times, he has won twice and "blondered" twice. Tomorrow will be the decider.

Afterwards, another record-breaking run: a whole thirty minutes non-stop. Arthur's postmatch exercise is of a different nature. If he sits down for too long he gets dizzy; so while I glide puffingly past the cow parsley dreaming of delinquent wives he walks slowly twice round the house to clear his head. "Zis Parkinson's, it knocks me sideways." His attitude to his illness seems mainly one of interest. He mentions other famous people who have suffered from Parkinson's. It is a distinguished disease (a disease for people with two houses, perhaps). His response to old age is also scientific and practical. The brain needs exercise like any other muscle. He writes five hundred words a day. He does the *Times* crossword. No doubt his chess games with me are designed not just for pleasure.

Domestically, he is a frail dictator. The telephone rings while he is in the house and Cynthia is gardening. Arthur gets up and walks slowly to the front door. "Ooo-oo," he goes, an Indian brave's call now reduced, in old age, to a squaw's call. "Telephone, angel." And Cynthia comes running from the garden. Neither seems to find this system unusual. One year, my wife and I are staying at Denston on Arthur's birthday. The telephone rings several times; Cynthia screens the callers. Perhaps he takes one birthday greeting out of six. Nor is there, for the rest of that day, any acknowledgment of the date. He is devoid of sentimentality or nostalgia. In the same way, he is interested only in what he is working on now, not what he wrote thirty years ago. In another writer this might spring from irritation at being praised for your backlist while doubts are raised about your current preoccupations; with him it seems quite genuine. He once showed me a garage at Denston which he mockingly referred to as his "archive": I remember rows of steel shelving and large numbers of foreign editions. "Do you have a copy of your first book?" (I remembered it as an encyclopedia of sex written under a rather transparent pseudonym.) "Of course not," he replied. "That would be an enormous vanity."

He is a very courteous man. I quiz him about his name being on a board outside the local church: there is "Arthur Koestler" amidst a lineup of English officers, gentry, and clergymen appealing for funds. "It is expected," he replies defensively and a little stiffly, as if I should not be so openly surprised at an agnostic Hungarian Jew taking up his squirearchical responsibilities. At dinnertime he always rises to pour the first glass of wine for everyone — with however trembling a hand. His courtesy, however, should not be mistaken for indulgence. "You won't mind if I slip away after dinner?" he inquires most evenings, almost as if it were your house and his tiredness were making him a bad guest. But when, after dinner, you attempt to bid him good-night as it is only a quarter past nine and your glass has just been refilled, he responds with a slightly firmer emphasis, "I think we all go to bed now, yes?" Yes, Arthur. He needs Cynthia to help him: he has a contact lens, for instance, which he is no longer able to handle himself; she puts it in and takes it out for him. No doubt he also doesn't want you sitting up and discussing him with his wife.

GAME 5

Six in the morning. High cloud and light summer air. Moorhens are processing from the pond to the cornfield; two young rabbits are rolling on their backs in a dustheap where an elm has been removed; tits and sparrows are already in overdrive, all motion and babble. Nature is parodying itself for a city dweller charmed by the simplest country sights; and the sound of Arthur's voice is in my head as I watch the exuberant, carefree, normal scenes. "Zis Parkinson's, it knocks me sideways."

It is our final game of the series, the decider. I am thirty-six and in full health; he is seventy-seven and very ill; the score is 2–2. Perhaps he will never play chess again. Perhaps I should lose, perhaps I should make a deliberate blunder. Like every chess player, Arthur delights in victory and loathes defeat: surely, out of gratitude for his writing, and out of affection, I should throw this last game?

Such reflections seem patronizing and irrelevant after only a couple of moves. Has any chess player *ever* thrown a match? Chess is a game of courteous aggression — and therefore very suitable for Arthur — but the courtesy and formality only serve to sharpen and focus the aggression. As Arthur's first attack develops, he immediately stops being a seventy-seven-year-old invalid who may never move p-K4 again; he becomes a ferocious assailant trying personally to damage me, to overthrow and humiliate me. How dare he! Gradually, I neutralize his first thrust, then begin a dogged pawn-march of my own. At first the maneuver is purely defensive — I push a pawn, he is obliged to retreat a piece — but its nature slowly changes. I realize that a huge advancing arrowhead of pawns with one's pieces undeveloped behind them is hardly recommended by any reputable chess strategist, but in this particular game the ploy seems unfaultable: with every pawn-move he is getting more and more cramped. His pieces are pushed back until they have barely a single square left to go to: in one corner, for instance, he has a rook's pawn, doubled pawns on the knight file, plus a knight in the corner square, all of which are locked up by a mere two pawns of mine. His queen darts out, but I lay a trap and plan my final push. I move a knight, which discovers a double attack on his queen. He must resign — yes, he must lose his queen, and then he must resign! I've got him beaten!

At this point an alarm clock goes off somewhere in the house. It is set for regular intervals throughout the day and designed to remind Arthur to take his medicines. Cynthia has gone out, so we set off around the house looking for the alarm, which is still buzzing. For some reason this proves difficult; eventually we track it down in Arthur's study and turn it off. He dutifully swallows a pill and we return to the board.

My inevitable feelings of pity and tenderness during this interruption do not affect my planned ruthlessness on the board. The game, after all, is serious (on move 7 Arthur attempts to vault one of his bishops over the top of a pawn; he doesn't spot the illegality, I point it out, he apologizes — "It's my eyes, you know"). Now we settle back into our chairs again. Yes, that's right, his queen is attacked by two of my pieces. There is no free square for it to run to. I must win! But then, quite unexpectedly, Arthur finds a place for his queen: on a square currently occupied by one of my pawns. Fuck! Damn! A blonder! Worse, I'm clearly due to lose another pawn (in fact, the two pawns cementing down his K-side corner). Ah well, nothing to do but push on. Arthur, having prized away one little finger of my stranglehold, is able to begin an attack; I counter by grubbing out some of his seventh-rank pawns with my rook. Queens are now off, we have one rook each, I have bishop for knight (good), but am two pawns down. Even so, I have chances, incredibly strong chances: a pawn on the seventh rank, defended by a rook, and with its queening square covering my bishop. Yes, I must surely queen, and then win his rook. How can this not happen? Victory soon! And yet, somehow, I don't manage to queen (I can't quite work out why not — his king just lolloped over and messed me up, I should never have allowed it). I lose rook and pawn for rook, and though I still have bishop for knight I'm three pawns down. Nothing for it. *Resigns.* 3-2.

Afterwards, despite the result, I don't feel as depressed as I normally

would: it has been a fluctuating, violent, eccentric game in which we both
had chances, and I played as well as I could. That Arthur won makes me
feel, in the circumstances, a more or less grudgeless admiration. An hour
and a half, a titanic struggle, and I feel shattered: what a testament to the
old fighter that he overcame the young (well, youngish) whippersnap-
per. . . . But this magnanimity in defeat is not allowed to lie undisturbed.
Arthur has the true chess victor's talent for rubbing things in: over dinner,
an hour or so later, he changes the conversation to remark wistfully, "Of
course, I am only fifty percent vot I vos at chess." I'm not exactly cheered
by this not exactly tactful remark. But a little later I am partially restored.
Cynthia says she can't remember when Arthur last had a series of daily
games like this—surely not since he played George Steiner at Alpbach.
That must have been interesting; what, I ask, was Steiner's game like?
Arthur, a small man, has a way of puffing up his chest like a pouter pigeon
at moments of pride. "He played like a *schoolboy*." Well, that's some conso-
lation. Oh, and did you tend to beat him, Arthur? More puffed chest:
"Alvays."

ANALYSIS

We oscillate, Koestler recognized, between *la vie triviale* and *la vie tra-
gique*. I was preparing to run the marathon; he was preparing to die. I failed
(well, the winter snow interfered with my training schedule—and besides,
in the end my application was rejected, probably because I put "journalist"
on the form and they decided they had far too many journalists running
already and didn't need any more coverage); he succeeded. We met over
chess, that trivial pursuit which refers to nothing else in life, to nothing
significant, and yet which engages our full seriousness. George Steiner,
who like Koestler covered the Fischer-Spassky match, strove in his report
to convey the powerful emotions involved in a chess match. What he wrote
is certainly unforgettable:

> The poets lie about orgasm. It is a small, chancy business, its par-
> ticularities immediately effaced even from the most roseate memories,
> compared to the crescendo of triumph in chess, to the tide of light and
> release that races over mind and knotted body as the opponent's king,
> inert in the fatal web one has spun, falls on the board.

Steiner had the grace (and humor) to add: "More often than not, of course, it is one's own king." Without this rider, sated Casanovas would probably have been rushing to the local chess club to try out a more passionate sport.

Later that year my wife and I went down to Denston. Arthur said to us quietly, "Here is a conundrum which I cannot express to Cynthia. Is it better for a writer to be forgotten before he is dead, or dead before he is forgotten?" We nodded, and I remember thinking, *Well, that's hardly a conundrum for you, Arthur, obviously your work is going to survive your death. . . .* Except, of course, that this was not his question. He was asking which was *better*.

In late February of the following year Cynthia telephoned. We had a long-standing arrangement to take them to a Hungarian restaurant; she was canceling for the second time in a fortnight. She said Arthur had the flu, and whenever he got mild secondary illnesses it made his Parkinson's worse. She sounded nervous and apologetic, but no more so than usual; we agreed to fix a new date when Arthur was feeling stronger. "We're not going to let you get out of this, Cynthia," I said.

They did get out of it. Four days later Arthur and Cynthia killed — or delivered — themselves. I was standing in the newsroom of the *Observer*, one Thursday after lunch, and saw it on a television routinely emitting Ceefax news. A journalist standing nearby glanced at the screen and commented with casual knowledgeability, "He killed her and then did himself in." I wanted to knock the journalist down, or at least insult him violently, but said nothing. There wasn't any point in being angry with the fellow himself (saying the first thing that comes into our heads on such occasions wards off the reality, denies that death will call for us too in due course); what made me angry was the realization that Arthur was finally passing into untender hands (FAMOUS AUTHOR IN SUICIDE PACT, etc.), that he would no longer be there to correct things, get annoyed, or even just laugh. He had moved from "Arthur" to "Koestler," from present to past tense. He had been handed irretrievably into the care of others: how well would they treat him? (No more accurately than he would have predicted. All his life Arthur had been sternly opposed to having children: the *Times* obituary, in its final paragraph, invented a daughter for him and Cynthia.)

The note Arthur left was dated the previous June — before I played chess with him. In it he spoke of his clear and firm intention to commit suicide before he became too enfeebled to make the necessary arrangements. He reassured his friends that he was leaving them in a peaceful frame of mind, and "with some timid hopes for a depersonalised after-life beyond due confines of space, time and matter and beyond the limits of our comprehension."

His death was exemplary, well managed, and, from the evidence, easy. Cynthia's death was, from the evidence, difficult, and causes problems. That she lived entirely for him nobody doubted; that he could be tyrannical was equally clear. Did he bully her into killing herself? This was the unmentionable, half-spoken question their friends came up against. I did not know him very well, but I seldom met anyone with less obvious romanticism or sentimentality; I would judge that a suicide pact would strike him as foolish, vulgar, and anachronistic. Indeed, I can imagine him getting irritated with Cynthia for wanting to join him: if his death, like his life, was to be part of a campaign, if it was intended to change people's minds about self-deliverance, what could be more counterproductive as propaganda than for his healthy fifty-five-year-old wife to kill herself as well? Which provokes the slimy follow-up question: if he didn't bully her into it, why didn't he bully her out of it? It seems to me that at this point speculation becomes impertinent, unless you can imagine yourself as a seventy-seven-year-old suffering from Parkinson's and leukemia and no longer able to rely on prolonged spells of lucidity. If you can do that, then I'll listen to you.

Cynthia, in the note she left, said that she didn't think much of double suicides as a rule. She wasn't a dramatic woman; she was shy, nervous, birdlike, capable of seeming in the same day both twenty-five and fifty-five. She moved awkwardly, like an adolescent unhappy with her body, who expects at any moment to knock over a coffee table and be sent to her room for doing so. I liked her, but her character evaded me: it was as if she would not show you what she was like for fear that something (what?) might happen to make her realize she'd been a fool for showing herself to you. On warm summer afternoons at Denston she used to clear the pond of weed, with a dog occasionally and unhelpfully at her heels. She had a long garden rake with a piece of rope attached to the end of the handle. She would throw the rake into the pond, haul it out with the rope, scrape the weeds off the teeth of the rake, pile them on the bank, and throw the rake back in. It looked a slow and awkward business. She herself looked awkward, liable to overbalance into the pond at any moment; but she kept at it with what looked a childlike doggedness. Splash, pull, scrape, pile; splash, pull, scrape, pile; splash, pull, scrape, pile. That last summer I played chess with Arthur she didn't clean the pond.

SISSELA BOK

Alva Myrdal

Peer Gynt: Who are you?
The Voice: My Self. Can you say as much?
— Henrik Ibsen,
Peer Gynt, act 2

"What happens if I can no longer explain anything?" This was the first complete sentence I had heard my mother, Alva Myrdal, utter that day in late June 1984. She suffered from aphasia that had come and gone for years. A brain tumor pressed against her language centers and grew slowly. Sometimes during the last years she had been mute for hours or days of intense, anguished headache; in between she had been able to speak with her customary subtlety and clarity. But now at last the aphasia had taken the upper hand almost completely.

I can't forget her eyes as she spoke. To the end they wanted to reach me, to share from within herself. Her glance was clear, appealing, direct. I felt the immense effort with which she sought the right word and her disappointment each time all was blocked and she remained mute.

Alva Myrdal's life had been predicated on the belief that it was possible to explain oneself and to explain human problems in such a way as to offer new scope for imaginative responses. If she could only explain some difficulty dramatically and fully enough and then suggest practical steps for meeting it, then how could people refuse to take action?

The impact of her first book, written with Gunnar Myrdal and published in Sweden in 1934, could only have encouraged this faith in the power of explanation. Entitled *Kris i befolkningsfrågan* [Crisis in the Population Question], the book created a scandal by linking a discussion of sexuality and family planning to proposals for social reform. Many thought it offensive for a woman even to sign her name to such views. Overnight my parents became the notorious "Myrdal couple." Meanwhile the book went into one edition after another. Its radical proposals regarding housing, education, family planning, medical care, and the rights of women and children were debated across the land, and its vivid portrayal of the abject living conditions of Swedish families led the government to set up commissions to consider the reforms the two young authors had proposed. Over the next decade most of these reforms were implemented, providing the foundation for Sweden's welfare state.

Alva played the same role of explaining and challenging when it came to school reforms, postwar reconstruction in Europe, the battle against illiteracy and hunger, and the risk of nuclear war. To the end of her life, she kept her faith in the power of words to galvanize debate and to bring about change. Even when she turned to the most intractable-seeming problems of human aggression and the mounting danger of mutual annihilation, she continued to advocate practical steps — not only in order to get changes under way but to combat the tendency to give up in despair that she saw as the greatest danger to survival. In her book *The Game of Disarmament: How the United States and Russia Run the Arms Race*, she acknowledged that she herself had come close to despair about mankind's incapacity to respond to the collective threat it faces; but she still insisted that there is always something, however modest, that each person can do: "Otherwise there would be nothing left but to give up. And it is not worthy of human beings to give up."

To be threatened with losing all recourse to words was therefore for Alva to become imprisoned in a silence she had never chosen. Not to be able to speak out, to take a stand, to suggest changes, or even to explain if she were cold or in pain — this would be to become alone with everything, perhaps to be tempted to give up. This prospect was what had caused her, who never feared death, a deep anguish since the first time she had felt aphasia take hold.

I was struck with panic when her words were blocked. I shared her anguish, but I was also afraid of not being able to keep up the contact that she already mourned as lost. And to be able to explain — this need had informed our talks during the last few years. She shared not only her thoughts but also her ever more insistent efforts to become clear about the shape her own life had taken.

Alva had never wanted to write her memoirs as long as she had the strength to work for other goals. Her life had long seemed to her self-evident and therefore self-explanatory. When she began to experience the need for personal explanations, it was already more difficult for her to write. With groping words she sought more and more urgently to interpret and decipher her life, and to reply both to uncritical admiration and to attacks she thought too harsh.

In one of the last letters she wrote me, she told of questions she had come to puzzle over more and more: "How . . . is one's fate shaped in interplay with other persons?" And "How do I become myself?" Now that she had lived so long, Alva wrote, she could see, "as in a fifty- or sixty-year-old rear-view mirror . . . the completely preposterous shifts that have taken place between what I have become and what I should have been able to, perhaps ought to, have planned." She had not nearly explained enough.

Outwardly she had had a public life that many found great, exemplary, complete. In 1982, her eightieth birthday had brought tributes and admiring summings-up in the media. The same year, she received the Nobel Peace Prize. Time after time she was named Sweden's most admired woman in national polls. But she herself did not find her existence exemplary, blameless, or — least of all — complete. She saw much that did not correspond with the public image, and she refused to see her life as fully realized. There had to be room to breathe. There had to be a chance to create anew. "How do I become myself?" was a question that concerned the present as much as the past.

I received no further mail from Alva after the aphasia had taken hold. In vain she tried to form the simplest words: her letters crept out onto the paper like indecipherable squiggles. Illness had vanquished her written language as well as her speech. The brain surgery she finally underwent did not help. When she spoke I could barely understand a few isolated words; no one could decipher her sentences. It was too late for explanations, too late for questions. "Forgive me," she said time after time. My rush of panic came once again in response. How could I show her that forgiveness was not the issue? Was it not I, after all, who should have found words for two?

During the two years of her life that remained, I could still sense in her insistent efforts to reach through the wall of her aphasia that same Alva Myrdal who once spoke out so vividly on so many subjects. But in her beating against that wall I had intimations, too, of a younger, equally determined but more hamstrung Alva Reimer whom I had never known. This was the young girl in the provincial Swedish town of Eskilstuna who ached to study and read and travel but who found all avenues blocked off. The town high school was only for boys. She had no money to travel or buy books. Even library books were out of bounds: her mother, the brilliant, artistic, but domineering Lowa Reimer, who had lost her two only siblings to tuberculosis and lived in fear of death, forbade her children to bring such books into the house on the ground that they might carry germs.

As for private schooling, Alva's parents had neither the money nor the desire to pay for it. Lowa Reimer thought that her daughter should be satisfied with her own lot in life. And Albert Reimer, her father, was equally unsupportive. A self-taught builder, active from early years in the social-democratic and cooperative movements and a passionate admirer of Strindberg and Rousseau, he saw no reason for her to want more formal education. His hope was that his five children would grow up to be farmers and perform the task he admired above all others: "bringing forth food for humanity." He revered learning; but, faithful to Rousseau, he had nothing but suspicion for the ways in which it was mutilated in schools and universities.

In witnessing Alva's refusal, even during her last illness, to give up trying to explain, to reach out by means of words, I came increasingly to wonder about that young girl in Eskilstuna. What was she like? What did it take, in her teens, to begin to break out of what she saw as stifling family prohibitions and a small-town existence where the bounds of her life were so narrowly drawn?

And then one October evening eight months after Alva's death, I heard that girl's voice. Sitting by candlelight at home after a day of teaching, I felt all grow still around me as I opened a package that had arrived that day from Sweden and saw the letters it contained. Alva had begun to write them at the age of fourteen, just when her schooling had come to a stop. They were addressed to a former teacher who later became the leader of Sweden's Quakers. Some years before Alva died, she had written to ask me if I wanted to see these letters to "the very handsome Per Sundberg whom I had idolized at a distance"; but by the time there was a chance for me to do so, she could no longer tell me where to look for them.

Now I had them in my hand. An archivist helping my father to sort through his papers had found them in a plastic bag behind a closet door and sent copies to me, knowing of my search for them. I began to read and did not finish until late at night. The girl who wrote them was as near as if she sat across the table from me and young enough to be my daughter. In her letters, I heard an alternately urgent and hesitant voice. She was writing to the one adult she thought might take her aspirations seriously, a man who represented to her the larger world of the mind and of spiritual growth; yet she had to tread warily lest she should presume too much.

The first letter, written in August 1916, begins conventionally. Somewhat stilted, written with impeccable penmanship, it conveys her apologies for not writing sooner. Then she launches into what is uppermost in her mind: "I have now finished going to school after having completed all the [seven] grades." She speaks of her teachers; she hopes, she says, that she'll be able to begin going to some other school in the fall. But then she comes to the books that she has been reading, and out tumble names that were obviously talismans—Zola, Schopenhauer, Strindberg, and his Swedish arch-enemy Ellen Key, the exuberant promoter of free love, family planning, and voluntary motherhood. The owner of a used bookstore, Alva explains, allows her to read to her heart's content. In the letters that follow she speaks of her religious struggles, of a tedious year in a commercial school, of friendship and love and hate, but most of all of her continued reading: Auguste Comte, Jack London, John Stuart Mill; Maeterlinck, Scheele, Renan, Voltaire.

She also attempts to describe the traits her friends find most striking in her: honesty, self-control, and powerful enthusiasms and antipathies that lead her to be ready to do anything for those she admires but to be quite mean to others, especially her mother. What pleases her most is that her friends find that she is above all utterly herself: "Ever since I read *Peer Gynt*, I have wondered whether I was myself." She is not of an envious nature, her friends have told her, and does not begrudge anyone anything, but she sees no reason why she should not have what others have. Finally, her friends find her less biased than most, something she has worked hard to achieve, and possessed of a strong will which she claims to have lacked altogether earlier. "Then I used to be stubborn but not strong-willed. Stubborn I still am, but not quite as much."

"No, this sounds quite unpleasant," the letter continues. And I put it down and wonder: Why should she think of this cluster of traits as so unpleasant? On reflection, I don't think she herself did; but at a time when girls were taught to be meek, humble, effusive, and long-suffering, she may have hesitated to reveal a different portrait—of someone with a will of her own who stood up to her mother, unable to see why she should not have, say, the education and the potential for an adventurous life that others enjoyed. Perhaps she also thought that it might appear presumptuous, even unseemly, for a girl to reveal that she wanted most of all to be herself, and that she wondered, like Peer Gynt, what that might entail. In Ibsen's play, after all, it was Peer who asked such questions, and Solveig who sat meekly and lovingly and patiently at home waiting for him to return from roaming the world in search of an answer.

In her letter, Alva immediately changes the subject: "I would rather talk about my plans for the future." But just as suddenly it is clear that she cannot go on. At that point, this girl, so willing to reveal her innermost problems and her troubling view of herself to her correspondent, makes an about-face. She withdraws into ambiguous silence. "But actually I have no plans for the future: they are too fantastic."

No more explaining. Her plans *were* too fantastic. They would sound naive or presumptuous if she so much as dared to set them down on paper. Here she was, a small-town girl with no money and no chance of going to high school, much less to the university. Yet somehow she longed to have a creative, adventurous life which would lead out into the world and make possible great contributions — and to do so without sacrificing the traditional feminine role that encompassed marriage, children, and being what Peer Gynt called "somebody waiting at home." She wanted to fulfill both Peer's and Solveig's ambitions.

For such a life she had no models. It was not just that she saw most women as being restricted to domestic roles; the few well-known women she admired for having broken out of that mold led lives that seemed to her too austere. Great women authors and scholars, as well as women who had fought for equality and liberty, had almost all been childless and usually also unmarried. For centuries, many women scientists, educators, mystics, and poets had either chosen or been forced into celibacy. In her own time, employed women were still routinely fired if they so much as married, let alone became pregnant.

As a result, Alva had to improvise and weave together the two roles as best she could. She realized that she had to begin early to lay the foundations for such a life. With no further schooling in sight, she took a job in the town offices at fifteen, operating the shiny new "counting machine" and helping out with the tax returns. She split her earnings between book purchases, contributions to the family income, and a savings account for possible education in the future. With her parents, she kept up near-constant, often quite dramatic discussions of her predicament. Over and over she explained her refusal to settle for the cramped life that seemed all mapped out for her. At last, after two years and with her savings in hand, she prevailed. Her father agreed to try to persuade the town school board to offer, for a hefty fee, the same courses to a small group of girls that boys received for free. And he succeeded. To be sure, the girls could not enter the school buildings, and the stigma rankled. But at seventeen, she was finally on her way.

And now the weaving together of the two roles could begin in all seriousness, for that same summer she had met Gunnar, then a lanky university student of twenty. He and two friends were spending some summer weeks bicycling in the countryside; having arrived at Alva's farm, they had asked her father if they could sleep overnight in the hayloft. At breakfast the next morning, Alva met them. She was deeply struck by Gunnar. Here, she thought, was an entirely new sort of person — superior, broad-gauged, with a playful genius that made whatever others said seem heavy and muddled. His laughter, his freedom, the depth she sensed in his thoughts, all drew her to him. He in his turn seems to have been equally struck — and for life — by this beautiful, merry, profound young girl.

When, summoning up all his courage, Gunnar asked her to do the unthinkable and come along on the bicycle trip, Alva amazed him by saying yes. She may never have acted so impulsively before. It was as if she knew this chance would never come again. Fortunately, she thought, her mother was in a rest home just then; it was easier to dupe her father with a tale of going to visit a friend for a few weeks.

Beginning with this journey, Alva had an ally who was on her intellectual level, someone who wanted to get out into the larger world as eagerly as she. He enchanted her more than she had thought possible. Why should she not succeed in joining the two roles — as active seeker in the world and as loving companion, perhaps later as mother — now that she was starting school with the prospect of joining Gunnar at the University of Stockholm as soon as she was through?

That the two roles would at times clash was something the young Alva Reimer could hardly discern as she started out on the life that would take her so far from Eskilstuna. She would come to know every twist and turn of the struggle to unite them; yet she would also experience the joy and the creative force of trying to do so in as humane a way as possible. The essential task remained the same: to keep looking for practical ways out and to keep asking the interlocking questions that no amount of explanation will ever suffice to answer: "How is one's fate shaped in interplay with other persons?" and "How do I become myself?"

Meeting Matisse

I will approach him from a distance, a respectful distance, but not in fact so great as might be supposed. In short, I will begin with the Misses Strachey, Lytton's sisters, the daughters of that remarkable woman whom I remember as being tiny, blind, benevolent, and black, Lady Strachey. She had borne a great many children and indeed more daughters than I ever met, but there were four—Pippa, Pernel, Dorothy, and Margery—whom I knew quite well. Meeting them, one felt always that they belonged to the nineteenth century, that they were part of a social and intellectual elite; they were moral, tolerant, highly educated, and possessed more charm than beauty. Morgan Forster, as I have been told, took them as models for the Misses Schlegel in *Howards End*. It was, one felt, a privilege to know them, but they were all in one way or another somewhat terrifying.

Dorothy, the one who concerns us here, was the least terrifying, although it could be unnerving to converse with someone who took it for granted that one would recognize a quotation from Bossuet or an allusion to Chateaubriand; she was also, I suspect, the most passionate, the most gifted, and the most enthusiastic of the sisters, and her novel *Olivia* will surely be remembered. She was a woman with strong political emotions: as a girl, when Dreyfus was convicted for a second time, she swore that she would never again have anything to do with the French. It was a rash oath, for a few years later she married a penniless French artist. They had one daughter, Jane Simone, who was very much a friend of our family. Like her parents she was tiny; she had her mother's slightly hunched back, her father's small black eyes, and a delicate articulation which made it seem that she had neither bones nor muscles; she was perhaps the most intelligent of all the Stracheys.

When, in 1934, the doctors advised me to spend the winter by the Mediterranean, I suggested myself as a guest of the Bussy family. For many years they had inhabited a small villa on the coast between Monaco and Mentone. And it was here, one Sunday morning soon after my arrival, that Dorothy remarked that she would not be surprised if Matisse were to come over from Nice in time for tea.

For me it was rather as though she had said: "I daresay Jesus Christ will drop in after lunch." I had been vaguely aware that Simon knew Matisse, but somehow I had not supposed that he would come round for a cup of tea as though he were an ordinary human being. For me, indeed, he was not an ordinary human being, but rather a very extraordinary superhuman being. I have compared him by implication with the second person of the Trinity; I will push the comparison no further than to say that in his painting there did seem to me to be a divine element, and if one may imagine a deity who worked in oils on canvas then he would have had to have been something like Henri Matisse. It will therefore be easily supposed that when the noise of opening doors and unusual voices informed me that I shared a roof with him, my emotions were formidable. Not that I could be at all precise in my anticipations; fate had placed me fairly close to ringside and I believed that I could recognize a champion at sight, but equally it had taught me that great men are great in many different ways. Matisse would clearly be gigantic, but he might also be a surprise.

He was.

When I opened the drawing-room door I concluded that there had been some silly mistake. The guest who was discussing the weather with the Bussy family was indeed a "fine figure of a man," comfortably plump, fairly tall, his person assisted by an excellent tailor, and altogether very carefully trimmed. But of any other greatness I could find no trace. The chance visitor whom I had so absurdly supposed to be Matisse might well be eminent in the world of insurance or real estate, but he could not, surely, be the creator of *La Ronde*. But here a difficulty arose. I knew what Matisse looked like, there were photographs, there was a self-portrait — and these, absurdly but undeniably, referred to the amiable philistine to whom I was now being presented in terms which left no doubt that I was shaking the hand of the Master himself.

The mind flies swiftly from one hypothesis to another. I realized that I was being crass. When Matisse explained that the average temperature of Nice was slightly higher (or it may have been slightly lower) than that of Mentone, there was some magic in his meteorology which I missed. If only I could rise to the height of his real meaning, that meaning which was too subtle for my apprehension, I should be enchanted. I tried to soar to his sublimities. It was hard work.

He soon forgot about the weather and turned to his usual topic, which was M. Matisse. I was not, and never became, a close friend; nevertheless, there were occasions when he did tell me something of his agonies. They were not the agonies of a creator; rather, they were the agonies of a dealer who held very valuable stock and felt that the market did not realize its full value. There were occasions when he alluded to the appalling fact that there were persons who had not understood that he was superior to all other painters. He did actually shed tears over certain well-worn and barely legible clippings, brought out from an inside pocket and reread with indignation. These were tears not of self-pity, but rather of pity for erring mankind which, with invincible ignorance, ventured to find fault with his art or — just as bad — bestowed too much praise upon M. Picasso, a painter of undoubted talent, but one whose pictures suffered from the irredeemable fault of not having been painted by M. Matisse.

Vanity was too feeble a word with which to describe the feelings of Matisse for Matisse. There was something candid, innocent, and sincere about his approach to himself which disarmed criticism — and, after all, that immense talent was genuine. But although the great man's adoration of himself was justifiable and, in its innocence, forgivable, nothing could make it an entertaining topic of conversation. The Bussy family, which had offered no comment until after I had met the Master, took the view that Matisse was the greatest living painter, the greatest living egotist, and the greatest living bore. Why then did they continue to receive him Sunday after Sunday? Partly I think because he was Simon's oldest friend (they had — with Rouault — been fellow students in the atelier Gustave Moreau), partly because sometimes one did get a glimpse of the real Matisse. For the Matisse with whom one attempted to converse chez les Bussy seemed like Henry James's poet — an unreal phantom who discussed trivialities downstairs while the real man was sitting in the room above writing immortal verse. Indeed, in a painter, such a division of the personality seems less improbable, for the art of painting is even further from the art of conversation than is that of poetry. Listening to Matisse talking about art and life, genius and talent, age and youth, all with particular reference to the Master himself, one could indeed imagine that the man of genius was somewhere else talking to himself in a pictorial language of almost incomprehensible beauty.

Of those sublime communications I heard nothing. Others who were closer to him may have been able to hear something in his talk as great as the things that he could say in paint. For my part, I was content and more than content when the Great Man could, for a moment, forget his greatness and chatter in human tones. This did occasionally happen, as when Matisse would reminisce with Simon and recall old stories of life and larks at the Ecole des Beaux-Arts. At that time, it seems, one was either a mystic or an anarchist. Simon had been an anarchist. "And what were you, M. Matisse?" asked Janie. Unfortunately, the remark reminded the Master of what he had become. He cleared his throat, filled his chest, and gathered around him an invisible cloak of sententious genius before answering that when he was a young man it had seemed to him that there were already too many people trying to put brakes upon the progress of humanity, whereas now. . . . "Now," interjected Janie, "it is you who slam on the brakes." The remark left Matisse spluttering in angry confusion. One would hardly have imagined from Janie's modest but masterly memoir that she would have been so impertinent, and indeed such interjections were very rare. On another occasion, irritated by the memoirs of Alice B. Toklas, Matisse remarked that Mlle Stein could speak with no authority concerning the avant-garde in France because she knew far too little French, and on this subject he refused to be drawn into further comments. But these little diversions from his usual theme did offer the hope that he could be interesting if not brilliant. And indeed one Sunday afternoon, forgetting himself in the happiest manner, he remembered something he had heard and seen. Could it have been in the South Pacific? And was it perhaps connected with the culture of pearls? It is exasperating, when such trivialities remain in the mind, that this sudden excursion, a simple and humorous narrative expressed without the slightest pomposity, should have vanished. We all agreed that it was a memorable afternoon and that he had been charming.

I have said enough, I hope, to suggest that, so far as my own observation goes, Matisse was better in his dealings with the muses than with his fellow human beings; perhaps one may conclude with a note on Matisse and the machine. This is hearsay, for when I knew him the great man was conveyed hither and thither by a chauffeur as befitted a potentate. But there had been a time when the Master himself was at the wheel. I gather that he never actually made the complete journey from Nice to Mentone (it was all of ten miles), since his progress was impeded by the fact that whenever he was approached or overtaken by another vehicle he pulled up on the sidewalk,

at the same time stalling his engine. Even in those days there was quite a
lot of traffic along the Côte d'Azur, so his progress was slow indeed. This
was tiresome, but the spectacle of Matisse turning upon a busy and sinuous
road, flanked on one side by a rocky wall and on the other by a precipice,
stopping dead sometimes upon the verge and sometimes in the middle of
the highway, and then starting again — either forward or in reverse — with
sudden impetuosity was too much for the nerves of anyone who loved
Matisse or painting, not to speak of those of his passengers. I was told that
he never had a serious accident. The Fates, no doubt, treated him with
proper respect.

One morning in May 1937, back from a year's study at Clare College, Cambridge, I sat reading *Gone with the Wind* in the New York apartment of my former Yale roommate Chester Kerr, wondering what to try next in the job line. A hoped-for spot on *Time* had fallen through. The phone rang, and the call was for me—from another Yale classmate, Henry McKnight, who was working at the *Herald Tribune*. He said he had heard from Dorothy Thompson, then a columnist for the paper, that her husband Sinclair Lewis was looking for a secretary. Why not take a shot at that? He gave me Lewis's phone number.

The Nobel laureate himself answered my immediate call and invited me for an interview that very afternoon. He directed me to an apartment on Central Park South.

McKnight had not told me why Lewis needed a new secretary, and indeed I was not to learn the reason until many years later, when Mark Schorer, who was writing Lewis's biography, told me what it was. I was dimly aware of some of Lewis's notorious capers, such as his fisticuffs with Dreiser, but I had no idea that he was an alcoholic, and that most of his scrapes were boozy. He had had to be hospitalized once, in 1935, to dry out. His drinking had ruined his marriage, and he and Dorothy Thompson had separated on 28 April, less than a month before my appointment with him. A few days after the split, a friend called Thompson to tell her that Lewis had disappeared. Experience made her fearful for him, and intuition put her right to work. She got a list of inns in Connecticut and called them one after another. Sure enough, she finally located him in Old Lyme. With him was Louis Florey, a professional stenographer whom Lewis had employed off and on for years. Son of an illiterate French-Canadian blacksmith, Florey had served, as Schorer would put it, "as drinking companion and audience, valet and bootlegger, at least as much as he served as typist." He told Thompson that Lewis had had a bad fall. She drove to Old Lyme and found Lewis in a frenzy of delirium tremens. Furious at Florey for having let things get so far out of hand, she fired him, and she drove Lewis to the Austin Riggs Center, in Stockbridge, Massachusetts. Although the sanitarium did not ordinarily treat alcoholics, they discovered he had three broken ribs and took him in. Schorer told me that Lewis was famous for swift and spectacular recoveries. Once, while drinking on a farm in the Michigan dunes with the *Chicago News* drama critic Lloyd Lewis and his wife, and Florey as well, he passed out in the midst of uttering a sentence; Florey hauled him to a bed; an hour later he reappeared, clear-headed and fresh, and picked the incomplete sentence up in the middle and finished it. And now, within days, he was back in New York, on the wagon, and — to my eyes, as I first met him — full of sparkling energy and great charm.

The first impression, as he walked ahead of me into his living room, sat down, and lit a cigarette, was of a thin man put together with connections unlike those of most human beings. All his joints seemed to be universal. His long, slender hands seemed to turn all the way around on his wrists. Wolcott Gibbs had once described his emerging from a car —"a tall man, getting up in sections." Next, piercing pale blue eyes, the bluer for being lashed into the pink face of a redhead. Thinning light-red hair, ill-brushed and tufted, over a wide dome of a forehead. Then, in better focus, terrible cheeks, riddled, ravaged, and pitted where many precancerous keratoses had been burned away by dermatologists' electric needles. Narrow, dry lips, and a slender chin. I would have sworn that he was hideously ugly until he started to talk, when his face suddenly turned on, like a delicate, brilliant lamp.

We talked awhile about Yale. A member of the class of 1907, he had been a miserably unhappy outsider as an undergraduate. He was pleased that I remembered he had been given an honorary degree at my graduation. He asked me if I knew a classmate of mine named Brendan Gill. I certainly did — and then I recalled that Brendan had persuaded Lewis to submit a piece, along with contributions from Thornton Wilder, Archibald Mac-Leish, Stephen Vincent Benét, and other famous Yale writers, for a centennial issue of the *Yale Literary Magazine*, of which Gill was the editor. Lewis obliged. Gill took the article back in his own hand to Lewis in Bronxville, where both were then living, and told Lewis that the piece wasn't good enough for the *Lit*. The notoriously enrageable author, charmed by Brendan's blarney, rewrote it. I was an applicant; I refrained from bringing up this risky memory. Suddenly Lewis broke off the interview and dismissed me — curtly, it seemed to me.

Oh my, I thought; that went badly. What next? I returned to *Gone with the Wind*.

Early the following morning Lewis called up and asked me to come back up to see him at ten o'clock. This time we talked about England, where I'd been studying, and about the American Legion, which was just then holding a convention in New York. He told me that his wife Dorothy had said the Legion was the first manifestation of fascism in the United States, and he had said to her, "Come on, Dorothy, this is the first chance these fellows have had to get away from their wives in years. Let them have a little fun." Lewis had put me completely at ease when, once again, he suddenly sent me away, now thoroughly puzzled.

He invited me back the next morning. He began chatting about what it was like to be married to a newspaper columnist, without any bitterness that I could detect; and went on about one thing and another. His phone rang. He answered it in his bedroom. Soon he came back, and he said, "John"— he was now calling me by my first name —"I have to shave and change for an appointment. There's a young man down in the lobby who's applying for a job as my secretary. Would you mind interviewing him for me?"

The young man, I was happy to be able to report, was hopeless.

It seemed, without anything having been said about it, that that chore had been my first task as his employee. After some more casual conversation Lewis gave me a month to learn shorthand — he suggested either the Gregg system or speedwriting — and to switch over from hunt-and-peck to touch typing. He told me to report to him after thirty days at a house he had rented in Stockbridge. (I hadn't the faintest idea that he needed the security of being near the Riggs sanitarium, in case he should tumble off the wagon.)

The house was a small, simple, shingled, summer-resortish cottage. Lewis had settled in a ground-floor bedroom, and the whole second floor was mine. A local woman came in to cook and clean.

I had barely had time to unpack when Lewis put in my hands the typescript of a novel he had just finished and asked me to read it and tell him
what I thought of it. I had no way of knowing that he had reached a critical
stage in his writing life. He was fifty-two years old. He had won the Nobel
Prize seven years before, at the end of a remarkably fecund decade, which
had seen the appearance of *Main Street, Babbitt, Arrowsmith, Mantrap,
Elmer Gantry, The Man Who Knew Coolidge,* and *Dodsworth.* He had
coveted the Nobel and had lobbied for it with shocking brazenness, but the
hanging of the medal around his neck in Stockholm had turned out to
mark, as the *Herald Tribune* put it, "his awful hour of nakedness." The
tirade of his acceptance speech on the poverty of American culture had
raised such a storm back home that Calvin Coolidge felt the need to say,
in one of his longer and more ornate sentences, "No necessity exists for
becoming excited." Lillian Gish told Schorer that Lewis had said to her,
"This is the end of me. This is fatal. I cannot live up to it." He had published
two mediocre but commercially successful novels, *Ann Vickers* and *Work
of Art,* and then, in the last flare-up of his astonishing creative energy in
his lifetime, he had dashed off the massive, awkward, but resonant novel,
It Can't Happen Here, in four months of work. That book had been published a year and a half before he hired me.

The typescript he handed me was entitled *The Prodigal Parents.* Ten
years earlier, bouncing back from the revulsion of *Elmer Gantry,* Lewis had
begun to plan a more positive novel with a labor leader like Eugene Debs
for a hero, who lived by "the God within" him. Its theme would be: "Blessed
are they which are persecuted for righteousness' sake." Again and again in
the following years, he had sought out one knowledgeable informant after
another, who could be for this work the sort of teacher and guide the bac-
teriologist Paul de Kruif had been for *Arrowsmith.* Nothing ever came of
it. After the publication of *It Can't Happen Here,* when Lewis had been
accused of being a communist, a young radical Dartmouth student named
Budd Schulberg invited him to Hanover to talk to some Marxist under-
graduates. They soon found out that Lewis hadn't a political bone in his
body, and they began to bait him, until he shouted, "You young sons of
bitches can all go to hell!" and walked out on them.

With *The Prodigal Parents,* Lewis turned his back once and for all on
the idealistic labor novel and instead took a petulant revenge on Budd
Schulberg's friends. The parents were a mawkish couple named Fred and

Hazel Cornplow, and their children were silly left-wing college kids who were taken in by a cartoon-page Commie. Even I — who knew none of this background — could see that it was awful. It was destined to receive some scathing reviews. Lloyd Morris would write that Lewis "has never been less of an artist." Malcolm Cowley would find the book "flat, obvious, and full of horse-play that wouldn't raise a laugh at an Elks' convention."

But I was twenty-three. Sinclair Lewis had won the Nobel Prize. I wanted this job. I had courage only up to a point — to the point of telling the author that he had got his students' vernacular all wrong. We went through the dialogue line by line, and I think now I must have helped Lewis to make his book a little more obvious than it already was.

Lewis's life was in a mess. But I was to have a marvelous summer, oblivious of his suffering. He never took a single drink while I worked for him; I remained in total ignorance of his history. I saw a surface that was gentle, kindly, boyish, and vividly entertaining. He treated me as a young friend, insisting that I call him Red. My work was fun. Taking his rapid dictation and reading it back to type it was like doing a crossword puzzle: I caught every fourth word with a squiggle of Gregg and had to figure out what went between. "If you want my autograph," he would dictate in a note to a fan, "you must send me a self-addressed envelope with a postage stamp on it"— chuckling at the idea that I would have to address an envelope and put a stamp on it to send the note. He wrote his new work on a typewriter, making many changes in longhand, and I copied the pages fresh. I was his chauffeur. One important task, every other day, was to buy a box of chocolates — no nougats in the fillings, no nuts, Louis Sherry creams preferred — to appease a liver which, to my unknowing, had been mightily revved up by his years of drinking. In the evenings, when he entertained at home, I was his bartender, serving his guests. When he was invited out, he asked his hosts to include me, and I sat in on evenings, thrilling to me, with John Marquand, Owen Johnson, Ellery Sedgewick, Jr., and others.

He was endlessly playful. "He could no more stop telling stories than he could stop his hair growing," Carl Van Doren once said. When we lunched alone, he would start a tale — either true or invented on the spur of the moment — and then, all for me, and of course for his own pleasure, he would jump up from the table and become the people in the story, switching from side to side as he conversed with himself in the telling. His improvisations were uncanny; one forgot his cadaverous face and *saw* John L. Lewis, FDR, Huey Long, Father Coughlin. He could reel off astonishing footages of Milton, Blake, Edward Lear. In company he organized games. Once with John Marquand and others he passed around pads and pencils and made everyone see how many names of rivers beginning with *M* they could write down. He would assign guests outrageous names from telephone books and tell them to converse in character with the names. He would hand out a set of end rhymes and get people writing sonnets with them against the clock; Schorer records that Lewis's own best time was three minutes and fifty seconds. He hired a small donkey one day when two very tall people were to be at the house; for some reason he wanted to see them riding around with their feet dragging on the ground.

Word games and letter games were his favorites. He rattled off tongue-twisters, spoonerisms, oxymorons. I must preface examples of alphabetic Jewish dialogues that he wrote down for me one day with the assertion that anti-Semitism was not among his problems; it horrified him. His incomplete works included a play, *Undiscovered Country*, about anti-Semitism in New York medical schools and hospitals, and a novel on the subject that he sketched out. Here, at any rate, was an exchange between a father and his son Abraham:

> ABCD goldfish?
> LMNO goldfish!
> SARA goldfish.
> OICD goldfish.

And a conversation with a waiter in a restaurant:

> FUNEX?
> SVFX
> FUNEM?
> SVFM
> MNX, please.

Apart from correspondence, my secretarial work consisted of copying draft pages of a play he was writing about the horrors of communism in an imaginary Balkan kingdom, Kronland. It was my secret knowledge that it was even worse, alas, than *The Prodigal Parents*. Lewis had long been stage-struck. His writing gift was mimetic, his ear a high-fidelity recorder, and he loved nothing better than to stand and recite to an audience, even of one, me, what his inner tapes had caught. He had collaborated with Lloyd Lewis on *Jayhawker*, a play about a roistering Civil War Kansas senator, which had lasted less than three weeks on Broadway in 1934; and he had written a stage adaptation of *It Can't Happen Here*, which had opened to mixed notices in simultaneous WPA productions in eighteen cities in 1936. In years after I worked for him, he would pluckily go on both writing for and acting on the stage.

A pleasure for him – and for me – was that because of this interest the house would be alive evening after evening with the chatter of the young actors and actresses of the summer theater in Stockbridge. "The theater fascinated him," his friend Marc Connelly would later write, "but I do not think he ever had any comprehension of its technical demands." During those evenings, in intermissions between parlor games, Lewis would endlessly ask primitive technical questions of the young summer-stockers: How do I get a character on and off stage in such-and-such circumstance? Does it matter if the speaker is upstage of the listener? Looking back, I think I can visualize better than I could at the time, in those gatherings, what Schorer would speak of as his "uncritical gregariousness and concomitant loneliness"– the disfigured redheaded Great Man with a second wrecked marriage whispering to his young secretary that he should make a date with the ingenue of the company.

A sure sign of his loneliness was to be found in his parade of guests, for meals and for weekends. He and I almost never ate dinner alone. One of the most touching manifestations of his kindness was his concern for my future as a writer. If a weekend visitor was to be the publisher Harrison Smith or the editor of the *Saturday Evening Post*, Thomas Costain, he would carefully instruct me on their fancies and foibles, so that I could most effectively ingratiate them, against rainy days to come.

During one of the visits of his warm friend Harrison Smith, I learned much of the story of Lewis's roller-coaster relationship with Yale. As an undergraduate he had written pieces for the two campus magazines, the *Yale Literary Magazine* and the *Yale Courant* – no less than thirty-seven of them; but of course this yokel, who thought nothing of walking down Chapel Street on a warm spring evening in his pajamas, was not chosen as editor. Called upon to make a speech at his fifteenth reunion, after *Main*

Street but before *Babbitt*, he said, "When I was in college, you fellows didn't give a damn about me, and I'm here to say that now I don't give a damn about you."

But drinking with Hal Smith in New York one day nine years later, he decided on a whim to drive to his farm in Vermont, and to stop off on the way and give his Nobel medal to the Sterling Library at Yale. The two set off in rough working clothes, and, as Smith told it to me, paused at a number of roadhouses on the Post Road on the way to New Haven to rehearse, over refreshment, the solemn ceremony of donation. Arrived at New Haven, they looked up Selden Rodman, an editor of the radical student magazine the *Harkness Hoot*, who had defended Lewis in one of its issues against a savage attack on him by an undergraduate named Eugene V. Rostow. Rodman took them reeling to the library. The librarian was out of town. A genteel young employee named Rush, confronted by what seemed to him to be two inebriated hobos, one of whom swung some sort of medallion back and forth under his nose like a pendulum, said with elegant diction, "You wish to see our collection of medals?" Lewis flew into a wild rage and stalked out, swearing never again to have "anything to do with any Yale activity."

Came, however, Brendan Gill, six years later. After Lewis's piece for the *Lit*, "Random Thoughts on Literature as a Business," had been polished to Gill's satisfaction and published, Gill kept on calling on Lewis. One day Lewis said he had been invited by an obscure Western college to accept an honorary degree. Wasn't it strange that Yale had never proposed such a thing? Gill told William Lyon Phelps about Lewis's question, Phelps told Carl Lohmann, the University Secretary, and Lohmann, who had heard the library story, shot Gill back to Bronxville to find out whether Lewis would accept a degree if it were offered to him. Lewis wrote Phelps:

> I'm very pleased to accept the Litt. D. degree, and I'm so writing Secretary Lohmann today. And triply pleased that it's you who are to present it. I suspect how many foul and secret plots you and that agent of the Yale O.G.P.U., Brendan Gill, have undertaken to accomplish this. . . .

In July of my summer with him came the tenth anniversary of Lewis's first meeting, at a press conference and tea party in the German Foreign Ministry in Berlin, with Dorothy Thompson, then the Berlin correspondent of the *Philadelphia Public Ledger* and the *New York Post*. The day after the press conference was to be her thirty-third birthday, and she invited Lewis to a party. Later she would write him about that evening in her apartment: "I will never forget how you looked, or how I felt, that first night. I felt a terrific indignation. I thought, 'My God, how he suffers.'" Lewis, evidently sensing that he might be given tender loving care by this dashing, energetic, and compassionate woman, proposed marriage to her that very night, and he kept repeating the proposal every time he saw her until, sometime in August, she accepted her role as his marital nurse. He told me once that *Dodsworth* was in part a replay of his pursuit of Thompson all over Europe. He talked to me about her a lot. He seemed to miss her, and each time we were to drive to Barnard, Vermont, to spend a weekend with her, he would have me take his clothes to the cleaners beforehand, and he would have a haircut, and on the road on the way up he would be in high spirits. Within an hour of our arrival, he would be fighting with her.

Lewis flew through life, a helpless missile rocketed along by some furious inner propulsion. "Is the wanderer like me homeless," he wrote during a honeymoon tour of England, "or does he merely have more homes than most people?" In the ten years after he met Thompson in Berlin he alighted — several different times in a few of the places, but always hurrying on to some inviting elsewhere — in Paris, Moscow, Sicily, Rome, London, New York, the New York suburbs, Vermont, ten towns in Florida, North Carolina, Toronto, Boston, New Jersey, Pittsburgh, Reno, San Francisco, Carmel, Los Angeles, Kansas City, Baltimore, Annapolis, Austria, Bronxville, Bermuda, and, briefly, the little center-cone of the twister where it had all started, Sauk Centre, Minnesota. Thompson was a vagabond, too, and during his peripatetic courtship of her, he had written to her promising that when they were married they would settle down on a farm in Vermont (of a sort the restless Dodsworth had yearned for), where they might at last find a pastoral inertia — a repose of spirit as well as body. Even before they were married she began shopping for linen for that imaginary haven.

On their first return to the United States they had bought Twin Farms, to which I was to drive Lewis for visits that summer, a three-hundred-acre place near Barnard, Vermont, with two houses on it, one a farmhouse built in 1796, the other a larger house perhaps converted from a barn. The following year they remodeled the latter, creating a huge, light-filled living room and a bedroom-study for Lewis. It was — for me — a heavenly place to visit. I had the old farmhouse all to myself.

Repose, sad to say, was not to be given to the Lewises. As Thompson went from success to success and Lewis from bottle to bottle, he apparently began to see his nurse-wife first as a nanny and then as some kind of malevolent tyrant. He complained that he had to share his marital bed with world affairs; he threatened to divorce her and name Hitler as correspondent; he said he felt as if he were married to a senator; and when her name was seriously put forward to run for president in 1936 he said, "Fine. I'll write 'My Day.'" Once as we drove away to return to Stockbridge, he cried out, "If I ever hear any more talk about Conditions and Situations, John, I'll commit either suicide or murder." In the evenings, during our weekends at Barnard, troops of witty young men like Joseph Alsop, Alexander Woollcott, and Vincent Sheean, and their friends, would sit on the floor in an entranced circle around Mrs. Lewis as she held forth after dinner, while Lewis — without the comfort of the brandy they were all sipping — would sit behind the curtain of a newspaper on the other side of the room, occasionally rattling the paper in outrage at something Thompson had said. At breakfast the next morning, he would pick up on one of these somethings, telling her she had had her facts all wrong on Yugoslavia, or John L. Lewis, or Franco. Then a few days later, in one of a series of her columns entitled "Grouse for Breakfast," he would have to read her mockery of his arguments.

I couldn't help being on Lewis's side. I must have been too young to recognize the bitterness of an exhausted gift, and of course I was ignorant of the drinking history. Dorothy Thompson seemed to me an overpowering figure in a Wagnerian opera, a Valkyrie, deciding with careless pointing of her spear who should die on the battlefield. Some things about my boss's home life, if it could be called that, did make me uneasy. Lewis's son by his first wife, Wells, then a Harvard student about to be twenty years old, was sometimes at Twin Farms, and Michael, seven that summer, was always there; Lewis seemed distant from both boys. I liked Wells, a rather shy and studious person, and I couldn't help noticing that his father seemed unable to talk with him. Michael made his father jumpy and irascible. I think Schorer must have got from Dorothy Thompson a report that at about this time Micky said, "I hate my father and when I grow up I'll kill him."

It was a relief to get back to Stockbridge, where Lewis's outward cheerfulness and playfulness were quickly restored.

No matter that Lewis's Muse was in menopause: I was fascinated by his habits as a writer. It was exciting for a kid who wanted to write to be around a man who lived so intensely by, for, and in his work. He would sometimes get up at two in the morning, brew up coffee, type for three hours, and go back to bed. He left notebooks all around the house, and he urged me to look through them, so that we — or, rather, he, before a dumbstruck sounding-board — could discuss possible undertakings. He said he needed to know everything about the characters and the setting of a story before he started writing. Maps of imaginary towns sketched in pencil, floor plans of houses, life histories, word portraits in the most painstaking detail, characterizing anecdotes, breeds of pets, dishes served at table, names of eccentric specimen shrubs that a particular character would be sure to have planted outside the house — there was an astonishing wealth of ground-work in those loose-leaf notebooks. Most of the material would never be mined. Waste didn't seem to bother a man with such a wealth of visual and aural memory and such speed of reference to it — and with such lack of pity for his own work. It would horrify me, as I endlessly retyped his drafts, to see thousands upon thousands of words — not scattered words and phrases but long passages, whole scenes — ruthlessly slashed out.

He doted on names; he believed people *became* their names. He had a stack of telephone books from all over the world, so he could find an odd but apt name for a character from New Orleans, or, if needed, a Roman, or an Alpine innkeeper. When he had to name a new character, he would make a list of a dozen possibilities and leave the list on the piano in the living room; day after day he would pick up the list and cross off a name or two, until he had made his final choice by elimination. I would some-times hear him at his desk calling out names, as if summoning lost souls.

In the autumn his feet must have begun to itch again; he wanted to be near New York theater people, and he moved back to the city, taking an apartment at the Wyndham, at 42 West 58th Street. I moved into quarters with my brother and five other recent college graduates and would turn up for work at the Wyndham at nine in the morning — once to find that Lewis had been up until five with the director Jed Harris and was still up, at his typewriter, in a fever of excitement over new ideas.

It began to be evident that he no longer really needed me. We didn't dine together now, and at lunchtime he would send me out to fetch him a take-out sandwich. (Once we did go out together in mid-afternoon for a snack. We wound up at a Longchamps. As we had sometimes done during the summer, we each had a doughnut and a cup of coffee. In Massachusetts the whole bill had been twenty cents; here, when the check came, I saw the rouge of rage bloom on Lewis's pocked cheeks. The check was for $1.57. Lewis said nothing, tipped the waiter, rose to leave. Near the door, where on a brass pedestal a large bowl of dainty mints of many colors stood, he reached down and scooped a double handful into his coat pocket. He went out with his head high.) I still served as his bartender during evenings when he had friends in, and it was then that I saw that my time with him was rounding out, for he took particular care to introduce me to people who might be helpful to my future: Irita Van Doren, editor of the *Herald Tribune* Sunday book section (for whom I did indeed later write reviews, my first signed pieces); John Gunther, whom Lewis urged to give me advice about journalism; Laura Hobson, then the advertising manager of *Time*, who might (and who, in fact, soon did) help me get a job at the magazine; Jed Harris, in case I ever caught stage fever (who years later did invite me to write a play for him); and others.

An even more explicit hint of my disposability took a bizarre form. The main point Lewis had made in his piece for Brendan Gill and the centennial issue of the Yale *Lit* was that it was getting difficult for a young person to break into print and earn a decent living by writing; therefore aspiring writers should first make a nest egg in some other line of work, which would then support a full life of letters. Lewis now preached this doctrine to me. He further had a suggestion as to a line of work. The year was 1937. War loomed, he said. When it came, he said, there would surely be a boom in the demand from small boys for lead soldiers. I should study the craft of their manufacture, make a pile, and *then* write my heart out. He was perfectly serious, and he even mesmerized me into going to F. A. O. Schwarz, Macy's, Gimbel's, and several smaller stores to look into the lead-soldier market. Try as I might to picture myself as a lead-soldier tycoon, I failed, thanked Lewis for his suggestion, and, having had a lovely summer with a vivid, brilliant, kind, driven, suffering man, I resigned, got from Laura Hobson the name of the person who was then hiring writers for *Time*, remembered with some asperity their having turned me down flat the previous spring, wrote a twenty-four-page essay on how rotten the magazine was, handed it in, and was hired the next day.

Charles Olson and an American Place

"At eight-thirty tonight John Cage mounted a stepladder and until 10:30 he talked about the relation of music to Zen Buddhism while a movie was shown, dogs ran across the stage barking, 12 persons danced without any previous rehearsal, a prepared piano was played, whistles blew, babies screamed, Edith Piaf records were played double-speed on a turn-of-the-century machine. . . ."

This journal note of mine, recording what is said to be America's first "Happening," is dated August 1952, Black Mountain College, North Carolina. I have long felt a need to pay tribute to this visionary community, and particularly to Charles Olson, the poet who guided it through its final phase with his maddening and towering presence.

Black Mountain originated in 1933, in the same decade of educational ferment in which Antioch, Bennington, Sarah Lawrence, and the University of Chicago designed their progressive curriculums. I signed up for my first summer session there in 1951, at the age of twenty, having gravitated to it for reasons that then seemed eminently objective: How captivating, in the span of two months, to study painting with Ben Shahn and Robert Motherwell, dancing with Merce Cunningham, music with John Cage, writing with Charles Olson. A dissolutely aesthetic adolescent, I was drawn to each of these possible vocations and several more; I had received one of those antiquated European educations which encourages young women to draw landscapes, play the piano, execute basic ballet steps as fluently as they read and write.

I arrived at Black Mountain straitlaced by many other conventions: the protocols of France's diplomatic corps and of its impoverished French aristocracy (my father's world); the decorum of my mother's fashionable salons and of my American schools — Spence, Bryn Mawr, and Barnard, where I'd begun a major in medieval philosophy. I brought these inhibitions to a community pledged to rebel against all traditional modes of behavior, in life as in art. And it took me a few months to realize that I had gravitated towards Black Mountain not for detached aesthetic purposes, but out of an instinctual need to purge myself of much ancestral folderol, to engage in that symbolic parricide without which none of us can become totally adult. It was with equally blind instinct that of all the alluring mentors Black Mountain was offering in the summer of 1951, I gravitated to the most iconoclastic and dictatorial of the lot, Charles Olson.

Charles Olson was born and raised in Gloucester, Massachusetts. After receiving a Ph.D. in American Civilization from Harvard (the first doctoral candidate in that department) he worked as a fisherman and a mail carrier between brief stints of teaching. He came to Black Mountain in 1949 at the invitation of the artist Josef Albers, then the rector of the college, and soon afterwards succeeded him as rector when Albers moved on to Yale. It now strikes me as odd that he was only forty-two when I met him; for he emanated an awesome, oracular majesty (in part innate, in part shrewdly cultivated) which one only associates with the most seasoned shamans. He was a mountain, a giant of a man, measuring six feet seven inches and weighing 250 pounds. Thick lenses floated above his walrus mustaches, giving his steel-blue eyes a perpetually ferocious, irate gaze. The balding pate of his enormous head was fringed with a mane of graying hair that flowed to his shoulders, like that of some Indian sage. Just before coming to Black Mountain he had lived in the wilds of Yucatan studying the Mayan culture, and a Mexican wool serape was magisterially draped over his huge shoulders, even when he was bare-torsoed on the hottest North Carolina summer day.

Nineteen fifty-one: Olson's rebellion against all traditional literary forms, his militant insistence on subjectivity, self-expression, self-exposure — these were the first aspects of his teaching that struck me as revolutionary. The confessional journal engaged in with full sincerity was an infinitely nobler art form, in Olson's eyes, than any of those courteous short stories published in the *New Yorker* which have been the model of our literary taste. There was much of American revivalism in Olson: Bear witness by baring your soul, be redeemed by the sheer authenticity of your individual emotions. The uniquely American ideal of "finding oneself" (a phrase whose equivalent might not exist in any other Western language) was expressed by Olson in the most native populist style: Each aspiring writer in his workshop must realize "what is his or her *ground*, get to that, citizen, go back there, stand on it, make yrself yr own place, and move from that."

So whenever Olson was pleased by a student's particularly intense self-revelation (I cite another instance from my Black Mountain journals) he slowly rose from his chair to tower over its author:

"*Si*, Victor, *si!*" Olson shouted. "You have it, Victor!"

And he glared at the newly loved writer with fierce affection. In the case of Victor, Olson's fancy was caught by this visceral line: "I finger my innards for the truth."

"*Si*, Victor, you have it!" Olson triumphed. And Victor was held up as the workshop's hero for the rest of the week, until another equally raw metaphor of self-revelation caught the master's ear.

Like all introspective writers who have theorized about their craft, Olson was obsessed by the loss of energy between the rich immediacy of our emotions and the relative poverty of our scripted words: "The dodges of discourse," as he called it, "the distinction between language as the *act* of the instant and language as the act of thought *about* the instant." His infatuation with the Mayan culture came from the directness of its hieroglyphic writing, whose signs "retain the power of the objects of which they are the images." There was also much neoprimitivism, much redneck Yahoo posturing in this Harvard-educated scholar who preached that we would not be free "until we have completely cleaned ourselves of the biases of westernism, of greekism, until we have squared away at historical time."

Olson proclaimed that traditional concepts of linear time must make way in our writing for an authentic American concept of "space." Stated in the very opening of his best-known prose text, *Call Me Ishmael*: "I take SPACE to be the central fact to man born in America, from Folsom cave to now. I spell it large because it comes larger here. Large, and with no mercy." The ideal contemporary text, in his view, was a "space-field" organized by an idiom of shared Americanness, an optimally direct, colloquial vernacular. As in his own verse:

It ain't dreamt until it walks   It talks   It spreads its green barrazza
Listen closely, folks, this poem comes to you by benefit of its own
   Irish green bazoo. You take it, from here.

The lectures Olson delivered in his writing workshops were equally iconoclastic and antilinear, random shards of culture as purged of any historical coherence as the elements of John Cage's Happenings (which Olson hailed as one of the glories of the twentieth century). His classes averaged four hours and could last six or eight, and sitting through them was like seeing an archaeologist throw a tantrum in a richly endowed museum. Within the span of one summer class we might be assailed by snatches of Sumerian history, of Fenollosa's theories on Japanese art, of Heisenberg's principle of indeterminacy; by passages from D. H. Lawrence's *Studies in Classic American Literature*, Dostoevsky's *Notes from the Underground*, Leo Frobenius's books on African rock painting, Pausanias's *Description of Greece* ("more valuable than Plutarch . . . because of its careful localism"), and from Ezra Pound's *Guide to Kulchur* ("just because it razzle-dazzles History"). We would be simultaneously assaulted by lines from the medieval poet Cavalcanti and the early Renaissance poet John Skelton, and from Olson's more recent idols — Blake, Melville, William Carlos Williams.

Olson's collagist approach to culture, his stress on the spontaneous and instinctual, tended to breed a mayhem of narcissistic mumblings among his students; it led to adulation of several texts as idiotic as Ezra Pound's *ABC of Economics*, and more self-expression than there were selves to express. Yet his presence was magically fructifying because he did not so much engage in Oedipal rebellion against contemporary fathers, which would become the curse of the 1960s, as in a reappraisal of revolutionary great-grandfathers: "Big O.," as we called him, transferred to us the momentum of his gigantic, archaeological curiosity for all forms of "immediate" discourse, past and present. The fineness of his ear had few equals in his generation. No teacher I've ever had put greater stress on tonal texture, on the notion that in all literary forms "it is by their syllables that words juxtapose in beauty." He forced us to realize that prose is only as good as it approximates the condition of poetry — that state in which not a particle of sound can be changed without upsetting the entire page. And the lines of classical verse he battered us with most frequently had a haunting, reductive musicality whose repetition would make anyone into a better writer — Blake's "Ah! Sunflower! weary of time!"; the medieval lyric "O western Wynd, when wilt thou blow / And the small rain down shall rain"; these lines from Marvell's "The Garden": "Annihilating all that's made / To a green thought in a green shade."

How did I fare in this scheme of things, an adolescent girl skilled at all Olson most detested—Aristotelian abstractions, European proprieties? Parachuted into this virulently Yankee, predominantly male community whose favorite mottoes were Ezra Pound's "Make it new" and William Carlos Williams's "No ideas but in things," I fared with mixed results. Several aspects of my brief past made me somewhat suited to Black Mountain: I'd been a pacifist leftie and World Federalist since my early teens, I was a tomboy who had always identified, in art as in life, with male heroes. Once in college, I'd concentrated so heavily on my philosophical abstractions that I'd never taken a literature course beyond freshman English, thinking I was smartass enough to read all of it by myself; and Olson thought that was particularly fine. "Girl," he'd say, pressing his five fingers hard into my scalp until it hurt, "if you get the highfalutin Yurrup and *poh-lee-tess* and stuck-up schools out of that noggin and start playing Gringo ball you'll be okay."

That was a lot to get rid of in two months. And I'd brought along some equally unsuitable possessions to Black Mountain: my first short stories, in which I was always an adult male facing situations I knew little about— my favorite persona was a middle-aged alcoholic actor seeking salvation in a Bowery church. Olson was equally capable of abysmal rudeness and of exquisite, ambassadorial courtliness; and I've always been grateful that he never assailed these texts' atrociousness publicly. He reserved his ire for our tutorials. "Girl," he bellowed at me after reading my trash, "this is pure shit! You're going to do nothing but keep a journal for a year, an hour a day minimum, come back next summer and show me what's in it!"

So I went back north and obeyed Big O. and kept my journal through the rigors of my senior year of college, where I'd changed my dissertation thesis from medieval themes to a more irreverent topic, "Kierkegaard's Views on the Demise of Christianity." Throughout that winter I scribbled recollections of early childhood in my journal, noting one incident curiously akin to the one I'd just lived through with Olson.

In Paris in the 1930s, at the wish of my father, who deplored the laxness of twentieth-century education, I'd been tutored at home from the age of five by a tyrannical governess. The two of us traveled once a week to a correspondence school where we were doled out lessons for the following week, Gallically rigid homework (memorization of Asian capitals and Latin verbs, codifying of sentence parts) which was hardly conducive to a fertile imagination. But when I was eight an unprecedented event took place — a new teacher came in and gave us the following assignment: "Write a Story about Anything You Wish." Filled with excitement and terror by this novel freedom, I began as a severe minimalist:

> The little girl was forbidden by her parents to walk alone to the lake at the other end of the long lawn. But she wished to visit a green-eyed frog who would offer her the key to freedom. One day she disobeyed her parents and walked to the lake, and immediately drowned.

THE END

"Pathetic dribble!" the Father stormed on his daily visit to my study room. "You dare call that a story? What will become of you if you never finish anything!" He grabbed the paper from my little desk and tore it to shreds. It was a May evening of 1939, fourteen months before he died in the French Resistance. My father had been the love of my life, and he'd warned me that I should never write again. Always these male censors, silencing, silencing me. . . .

During my senior year at college I also returned, in my journal, to impressions of the past summer at Black Mountain:

Supercool pose of silence or monosyllabic utterances, bare feet, men's dark glasses and long hair, easygoing nudism and bisexuality — fads of the just nascent Beat Generation, precursors of the 1960s Movement style. (I hadn't skimped on Black Mountain's brand of unisex macho, chopping off my hair as short and jagged as a contemporary punk's.)

Everyone aping Olson's Yankee-phonetic spellings and punsome divisions: waz, enuf, luv, kulchur, yrself, lawd, abt, ga-wan for "go on," Ruman-tick, egg-zack-tly. All taken secondhand from 1920-vintage Pound.

The girl who danced in front of the mirror in the main hall from 7 A.M. to suppertime, stopping only to feed the baby braying in a basket by the exercise bar. She did not take any courses, she never spoke to anyone, she simply moved for about ten hours in a row, staring at herself in a mirror.

Olson, a serape flung over his naked torso, sitting in the dining room next to John Cage, always most formal in a black city suit and tie and very shiny pointed black shoes, punctuating the cultivated laconism of dinnertime with his tinkling, Zen monk's laugh as he mused about his next Happening.

Accompanying the poet Jonathan Williams to the Asheville, North Carolina, draft board in 1951 when he refused induction into the United

States Army on grounds of conscientious objection. That was as important a moral and political education as any I had received from family or college.

I returned to Black Mountain in 1952 for another summer session, as Olson had bidden me to, and showed him my journal. There followed a few treasured days when I was the Victor of that season's workshop, then reduced to six students. The first week of the seminar, Olson towered over us, glowering through his thick spectacles, his finger poised on a stark line of my journals. It had to do with my father: "I pointed westward, towards his grave."

"*Si, si,* girl! That's *space!*" Big Charles triumphed. "*Si,* you've got it, kid!"

But I didn't remain in favor long. For I'd brought Olson some other texts to read: three very autobiographical stories about my childhood which had followed his dictate to "Concentrate on what you know about, Write from the Center." Clearly inspired by my obedience to Big O., they had won me the annual Creative Writing Award given to a graduating senior at Barnard. Five hundred dollars, a tidy sum for those years, and all the ego trips such mini-honors bring. But Olson didn't give a damn about jurors from fancy New York publishing houses doling out prizes at a Big Sisters school. He was pioneering a counterculture, and such details made him all the more hostile. Once more he raged at me during a tutorial, shouting: "You're still writing conservative junk! If you want to be a writer keep it to a journal"— the giant walrus rising from his chair, all six-foot-seven of him towering — "AND ABOVE ALL DON'T TRY TO PUBLISH ANYTHING FOR TEN YEARS!" More censorship into silence; this time, perhaps, for the best.

I remained, as ever, an obedient daughter. I again followed Big Charles's advice. I kept my journal in New Orleans while following a jazz clarinetist on the rounds of Bourbon Street; in the dawns of New York when I relished being the only woman on the overnight shift at United Press, wrote World-in-Briefs about Joseph McCarthy's purges, drank martinis with my colleagues at 8 A.M. in sleazy bars under the Third Avenue El. I remained loyal to it throughout a myriad of other transient aspirations that all protected me from the fear of Becoming a Writer — flirting with the notion of entering Harvard's architectural school, or going to Union Theological Seminary for a degree in divinity. I persevered with the journal throughout my most misguided phase, when I earned my living in Paris as a fashion reporter, and dallied with a succession of consummate French narcissists to whom I eventually gave their literary due. I continued to write it after my return to the United States and my marriage, when I realized one of my life's earliest dreams and spent five years as a painter of meticulous landscapes and still lifes. For my Black Mountain guru had offered me an important metaphor: journal-keeping is comparable to the process of sharpening a pencil; our emotions, and the power of their expressions, are kept at maximum intensity by the daily routine of being inserted into the journal's sharpening edge.

By 1962 I had two children. I lived in deep country and in relative solitude, encompassed by domestic duties. The journal was becoming increasingly voluminous, angry, introspective. The nomadic tomboy, finally denied flight and forced to turn inward, was beginning to explode. One winter day I felt an immense void, great powerlessness, the deepest loneliness I'd ever known. I wept for some hours, took out a notebook, started rewriting one of the stories that had won me my college award. It was the one about my governess. It was published shortly afterwards in the *New Yorker*, precisely one year past the deadline Charles Olson had set me. Twelve years and two books of nonfiction later, it was to become the first chapter of my first novel, *Lovers and Tyrants*. The process of finishing that book entailed a solid and delicate psychoanalysis which forced me to accept my father's death. Epiphany achieved, I was able to write the novel's last three chapters — my first serious attempt at fiction — in a mere six months.

I may have had to bury the first Censoring Father to set my tongue free. I may have had to go to Black Mountain to bury many grandfathers, many mothers. I may have had to abide by Censor Two, Charles Olson, to let my tongue speak with any measure of integrity.

"A frontier society sometimes raucous and raw," so Martin Duberman would describe it in his fine book *Black Mountain: An Experiment in Community*, "bold in its refusal to assume any reality it hadn't tested, and therefore bold in inventing forms, both in life styles and in art."

Charles Olson attempted to keep Black Mountain alive during the last five years of its existence through the sheer force of his personality, with total disdain for all administrative detail. He was a tortured man who had talked like a puritan about "clean writing" being solely produced by "clean experience," and left his wife and baby to marry a student whom he had gotten with child. It was the way he had treated many women throughout his life, and I suspect he had too much decency not to feel his guilt, which he allayed by bouts of severe alcoholism after Black Mountain's demise. By the time I wrote him to thank him for inspiring my first published texts, in the mid-1960s, he was too far gone to answer. Charles Olson died at fifty-nine, a great talent which may never have found its true center.

His leavening influence on American literature can still be felt by reading through the *Black Mountain Review,* founded by Olson and Robert Creeley with the intent of loosening the grip of the New Criticism. It provided more fascinating reading, for my money, than *Partisan Review, New Directions,* or any other classy periodical of the 1950s. In its last number, dated 1957, one finds Allen Ginsberg's *America,* Kerouac's *From October in the Railroad Earth,* poems by Gary Snyder and Michael McLure, a section of William Burroughs's then-unpublished *Naked Lunch,* and part of Hubert Selby, Jr.'s also-unpublished *Last Exit to Brooklyn.*

Notwithstanding Olson's demanding, oppressive presence, the more gifted writers of the community he nurtured were able to avoid all sectarianism. Of the ten poets since categorized as the "Black Mountain School" (a term originally coined by an outsider, Donald Allen, in his 1960 anthology, *The New American Poetry*) only six had some connection with the college. Others had simply published in the *Black Mountain Review.* And the vast range of stylistic differences among the writers indebted to him — be it Joel Oppenheimer's domestic lyricism, Jonathan Williams's pungent sparseness, Fielding Dawson's Joycean memoirs, or my own discursive prose — makes the very term *school* ridiculous. Olson himself had clearly spelled out the terms of Black Mountain's adamant individualism: the writer "is not free to be a part of, or to be any, sect. . . . The poet can not afford to traffick in any other sign than his own, his self, the man or woman he is."

Few communities of its modest size — it seldom exceeded 120 in any given year — were ever nurtured within two decades by so distinguished a group. In addition to the ones already mentioned, it included Edward Dahlberg, Buckminster Fuller, Paul Goodman, Robert Creeley, Aaron Siskind, Stan Van Der Beek, Jasper Johns, Robert Rauschenberg, Cy Twombly, Kenneth Noland, Willem de Kooning, Arthur Penn, Alfred Kazin, Robert Duncan, Walter Gropius, Stefan Wolpe, and Franz Kline, among many others. But this proliferation of stars led Black Mountain to a very incongruous self-image: while trying to remain the City on the Hill, it saw itself both as a frontier and as a frontier salon. There were also the contradictions of its last rector: Olson's Black Mountain was obsessed by its unique and redemptive Americanism and by a totally opposite nineteenth-century Romantic vision of the artist as pristine prophet — Olson's favorite dictum was "Only the artist is on time." How to reconcile this narcissistic sacralization of art with a community dedicated, in good part, to abolishing all traditional barriers between art and life? "Write as you breathe," Olson always taught. "I want to erase *all* differences between art and life," Cage said. "Rauschenberg just wants to fill in the gaps between the two, which strikes me as a little too Roman Catholic."

Like Brook Farm, Oneida, and most other Utopias ballasted by a belief in their redemptive purity, Black Mountain would eventually founder on reality's edge. By 1955 the few dedicated faculty members who had remained had not drawn salaries for a year, and many had used up their personal savings. Olson's attempts at economic revival were of a tragicomic nature. He tried to get approval from the state to enroll Korean War veterans, and the college's remaining six students rushed from class to class, changing disguises every few minutes, to convince Veterans Administration inspectors that the community was thriving. A few months later, Black Mountain decided that despite its "principles" it would accept the mentally retarded son of a wealthy Southerner who had suggested that he might put some money into the community. The father was to fly his private plane over the college and dip its wings in a certain way to make it known that he had decided to offer a bequest. For a few days members of the saving remnant spent their time wandering about the fields, staring at the sky and waiting for the sound of a plane which never came. One can think of few gifted men put to such an absurd task.

I don't fully understand Olson's magnum opus, *The Maximus Poems*, but I believe he has an important, underestimated place in American letters. He left many fascinating essays ("Projective Verse" and the collection *Human Universe*) and a remarkable book on Melville, *Call Me Ishmael*, a classic of engaged, iconoclastic criticism comparable to William Carlos Williams's *In the American Grain*. His legacy went beyond published texts. I do not adulate Olson or Black Mountain the way most of its members have, feeling ambivalent about the sham and the magnificence of the man, the dangers and the vision of the place. But I thank him every week of my life for his prophetic emphasis on the valor of subjectivity and candor, of disobedience against form and state; and also for that fatherly rigor which eventually enabled me to write at all.

Decades later, as a woman nurtured by twenty years of feminism, memories of Black Mountain and Charles Olson still make me worry about the constant temptation, and great hazards, of remaining dutiful daughters. And they lead me to muse on these bittersweet paradoxes: how certain male mentors can force us to acknowledge our femaleness; how some male oppressors, by teaching us to rebel, may eventually become our liberators.

Alan Jay Lerner: Words and Music

There is a class of human being—an astonishingly underpopulated one, come to think of it—that can be made inordinately happy by the right rhyme couched in some nonsense verse, or by a common sentiment, naively expressed. They will kill for:

> And bound on that journey you find your attorney (who started
>   that morning from Devon);
> He's a bit undersized, and you don't feel surprised when he tells
>   you he's only eleven.

Die for:

> Hindoos and Argentines sleep firmly from twelve to one.
> But Englishmen detest a
> Siesta.

They will sacrifice all for:

> I've got a lunch that's planned which is
> Sandwiches and beans.

Weep at:

> Take back your mink—
> Those worn-out old pelts—
> And go shorten the sleeves
> For somebody else.

And rabidly froth at the mouth for:

Ev'ry time we looked around
There he was, that hairy hound
From Budapest.
Never leaving us alone,
Never have I ever known
A ruder pest.*

They are called lyricists, and they know how it feels to have wings on their heels. They think nothing of spending sleepless hours, days, or weeks searching out a line like "Oh, what a beautiful morning" or "I could have danced all night."

What is best about them is that they know they are not John Milton, nor do they aspire to write *The Waste Land: The Sequel*. But in the simple, fatuous grandeur of the moment when one of their actors (buoyed by a breathlessly ambitious cast, mired in Broadway's entrepreneurial greed, scarred by the critic's lash) steps into a pool of light and utters, "I've grown accustomed to her face," and there is, miraculously, genuine emotion felt — even as the lawyers hover in the wings, waiting to screw everybody out of their money — from the sheer surprise and purity of the feeling, over and against all the attendant vulgarity, the lyricist enters (briefly) Heaven.

Alan Jay Lerner was Chairman of the Board. Rich to start with, Harvard-brilliant, finished and educated to perfection, an incurable romantic and romancer, married seven times ("I guess it's just my way of saying good-bye"), from *Brigadoon* and *Paint Your Wagon* through *My Fair Lady*, *Camelot*, *Gigi*, and *On a Clear Day You Can See Forever*, he was perhaps the best we've ever had. Why? Because, like Cole Porter, he glittered in French; he had the technique and edge of Lorenz Hart; he could be wonderfully plain and make you cry, like Oscar Hammerstein; he had an extraordinary gift for title lines, like Ira Gershwin; and with all of that, he could lose Alan Jay Lerner completely and, like Frank Loesser, creep inside a flower girl's mind — or a knight's, or a housewife's — and make you believe the

---

* W. S. Gilbert and Arthur Sullivan, "Nightmare," from *Iolanthe*; Noel Coward, "Mad Dogs and Englishmen," from *The Third Little Show*; Richard Rodgers and Lorenz Hart, "Mountain Greenery," from *The Garrick Gaieties* (also from *The Girl Friend*); Frank Loesser, "Take Back Your Mink," from *Guys and Dolls*; Alan Jay Lerner and Frederick Loewe, "You Did It!" from *My Fair Lady*.

words they are singing are thoughts occurring to them at this very moment *now*.

When I first encountered his work I was thirteen, going to see my first Broadway musical — *My Fair Lady*. Lerner was further from me than the moon. Seventeen years later, a musical I had written had been optioned by Herman Levin, the producer of *My Fair Lady*, and Lerner was a phone call away. Levin and I were in his offices at Forty-ninth Street and Madison Avenue when he noted that Lerner was due back in New York and would likely be in his own offices downstairs in the building.

"He really should hear your score."

The hand went to the phone, and five minutes later, in he walked.

Short, gray, wrinkled, ravaged. The face was ravaged. I had met Richard Rodgers the year before. Also ravaged. What was it about a life of doing Broadway shows? Was this a warning? Lerner sat, fidgeted, kept pulling at a white glove on one of his hands, taking it off, putting it on. I later learned it was there to prevent him from biting his nails and cuticles. He sat; I played and sang. Every good line registered. He would drop his head an inch and shake it back and forth, as if to say, "Got it." His reaction to the music was physical. He was dapper and neat to look at, and arranged in straight lines; but the body moved in curves as if compelled from deep within, and the eyes were transported. In fact, they were the first eyes I'd ever seen truly transported by music. And then I got it. He didn't give a damn about the lyrics. For him it was all the music. The guy is a *composer* who doesn't write music but for whom the very fact of music is a kind of miracle. And when he hears it he's got to do something, and he does it with the passion and compulsion of a composer, except his stuff is words.

I finished and he said, "Terrific." Then he took me aside and the magic began. "When I was young," he said, "Oscar Hammerstein told me to come by his place from time to time to show him my work, and for him to give me some friendly advice. You come to my place from time to time so I can do that for you."

Chills. I was stunned.

We set it up for the following week. His office. All week I strained to find a gift I could bring to return the favor. Something I could come up with that would open music for him in a new way. After all, here I was, a professor of music theory, analyzing romantic Lieder daily. Surely I could find some wonderful relation of tone and text in Lerneriana to show him how good he was.

The answer was "I Could Have Danced All Night." Using Schenkerian analysis (Heinrich Schenker was an Austrian music theorist who had developed arcane techniques of music analysis then known mostly to graduate students), I could indicate how the long-range harmonic scheme of the song, through the end of the bridge, arpeggiated the tonic triad: C major, E major, G major, and finally C major. Further, the long-range bass motion was an enormous rhythmic extension of the opening motif of the song: C, E, G, c. Further, the completion of the large arpeggiation at the end of the bridge is brilliantly matched by the words, "I only know." Lerner, with his layman's ear — or so I theorized — had brilliantly perceived what the underlying musical structure was. He mirrored the musical structure with a lyric that moves Liza Doolittle from doubt to certainty about her changed feelings toward Higgins. By the end of the large-scale arpeggiation we know, from the music as well as from the text, that the two can never again be quite the enemies they'd been. Now, how to tell him? The problem was how to avoid technical terms like *submediant* or *dominant chord* but still to characterize the musical form sufficiently for him to understand the marvelous subtlety of his own work.

The day arrived. Lerner was all kindness, wrapped in a bundle of nervous energy. His office was small — a window, a large desk strewn with papers. On the walls some new melodies by Burton Lane, handwritten on score paper, were pinned to corkboards. He and Lerner were collaborating on a new show, and Lerner (I surmised) stared at the melodies until the lyrics occurred to him. I was afraid to ask how he actually did it.

He talked about my work, about what he liked and why. He spoke a great deal about what to do with good work and good ideas. "If it's good, always ask if perhaps there should be more."

That perked me up.

"*Gigi*, for example, came out of some songs left over from *My Fair Lady*." He paused for that to sink in. "Both Cinderella stories."

As he went on, I began to understand what I had been invited to learn. His lyrics, after all, were available in sheet music and on records and could be studied. His critique was wonderful, his private anecdotes revealing and instructive. But more valuable than any of it was simply being there and watching him in his world — the music on the walls, the glove, the desk, the window. He was letting me glimpse into the studio to see how he held the brush, how he studied the light, how he went about being a professional lyricist. It helped.

I owed him one. "You know, I've been thinking," I began slowly. "You did an amazing thing in 'I Could Have Danced All Night.'"

A puzzled look.

"I mean, the way your lyric matches an extraordinary hidden relationship that grows out of the music's organic form."

He leans forward. I begin talking about triads. "You see, each piece is in a key, and each key has a triad, and each triad has these notes, and the song does an amazing thing, going from C to E to G, like the melody — except by changing key. . . ."

Lerner stops me. "Well," he says, "you know Fritz [Loewe] is really steeped in the Viennese school of composition, and it would be stylistically typical of that school to modulate to the mediant major."

Right. Just my point. Except I was now sitting on it. I should have known from the music on the walls. I should have known from my first impression that he was a great composer in every respect save that he did not write music (an impression I felt even more strongly about Fellini when I later met him).

That was the first and last meeting. Lerner moved to England. He died last year. He was good, really good, and there should have been more.

BAYARD RUSTIN

Mr. Randolph

In my fifty years as a social and human rights activist, I have met and worked with some of the leading figures in the struggle for justice — Gandhi, Norman Thomas, Martin Luther King, Jr., Lech Walesa. But the man who most closely touched my life, whose ideas, character, and work helped shape my destiny, was Asa Philip Randolph, this country's premier black labor and civil rights leader. I have chosen to write about Mr. Randolph for two reasons. First, our association was a long and fruitful one. I had the privilege and good fortune of working with Mr. Randolph from about 1939 until his death in 1979 at the age of ninety. Second, though much heralded in his time, Mr. Randolph and his ground-breaking achievements in the struggle for racial and economic equality have been obscured by the passage of time. This was a man whom every major civil rights leader, from Roy Wilkins to Martin Luther King, affectionately and respectfully called "the Chief."

Mr. Randolph was, in the truest sense of the word, a pathfinder. Tall, aristocratic, with just a touch of vanity about his appearance, he was an intellectual imbued with unflappable dignity and courage, who used his outward reserve and quiet demeanor as a potent weapon in the formative years of the civil rights struggle. As a member of the Socialist Party, he ran for New York Secretary of State in 1922 and received an impressive two hundred thousand votes. Three years later, he organized the Brotherhood of Sleeping Car Porters. In subsequent years, he tangled with corporate executives, presidents, and this country's most powerful labor leaders, and more often than not, his dignity and steadfastness won concessions that paved the way for black social, economic, and political advancement.

Confronted with the humiliations of racism, insults, and resistance, he never lost his poise, and he never lost his nerve. He was imperturbable and implacable in his single-minded commitment to his ideals and principles. He was a self-made gentleman and a prudent tactician with the grit and toughness of a boxer. Mr. Randolph was a man of quiet courage, of resoluteness without flashiness, of perseverance without pretension.

Many of these attributes were evident to me at our first meeting, which occurred in 1938 when I was a student at the City College of New York. I had shown a friend of mine a paper I had written in which I concluded that the Communists were the only party sensitive to the needs of blacks. Now this was the time of the Scottsboro trials, in which the Communists were actively involved. Well, my friend disagreed with my analysis, and asked me if I had ever met A. Philip Randolph, a socialist who was firmly anticommunist. Of course I had heard of Mr. Randolph, but never met him. After some discussion, my friend suggested that we arrange to visit Mr. Randolph at the Brotherhood of Sleeping Car Porters headquarters up on 125th Street in Harlem. I was sure that a man of Randolph's stature would not bother with two young and unknown college kids.

Much to my surprise, we got a call from Mr. Randolph's secretary, who told us that he would see us. At that initial meeting, Randolph did three simple things that I saw him do countless times during our long association, and which illustrate the decorum and gentility that characterized his dealings with people and which, I feel, were a small but integral part of his successes.

When we arrived at Randolph's modest offices for our appointment, it was clear that he was busy and running late. But rather than just keep us waiting, we heard him come over to the door and tell his secretary, loud enough for us to hear, "Tell the two gentlemen from City College that I will be a little late." For years and years, when Mr. Randolph had to keep someone waiting, he would either send his secretary or come out in person and explain the delay. The courteousness and thoughtfulness made quite an impression on me.

The second thing that really impressed me happened as we were ushered into Mr. Randolph's office. This important man, instead of sitting smugly behind his desk waiting to receive us, got out of his chair, walked toward us, and shook our hands. He then did something which seemed most unusual. As he showed us to two seats near his desk, he gestured with his hand for us to sit down, but not like most people do by merely pointing to the chair. He made a gesture as if he were brushing or dusting the seat before we sat down, something I also saw him do for years and years.

Although these displays of civility may seem like insignificant and even overly obsequious acts, they were not. I later realized that it was Randolph's courtliness, his staid manners and reserve, that made it so extraordinarily difficult for opponents to dismiss him. In fact, his restrained manner was often totally disarming; it was a type of moral judo that threw opponents, including presidents and other officials, off balance. Although these qualities were an innate part of his personality, they were also an effective tactic.

At that initial meeting, Randolph discussed his socialist beliefs, outlining his positions on child labor, the six-day work week, trade union rights, black economic progress, and other matters. I was awed by his eloquence, his equanimity, his bearing, and his grasp of the issues.

I was so taken with Mr. Randolph after that first meeting that a year later I went to work for him in his major campaign to organize a march on Washington to press for an executive order banning segregation in defense plants. During the planning stages of the effort I got to know Randolph better. And he told me a remarkable story of a negotiating meeting between the Brotherhood of Sleeping Car Porters and the Pullman Company which further underscored his style and shrewdness.

Although always mindful of his dignity and decorum, sometimes Randolph let other, more indelicate spokesmen take the floor when things got nasty or when blunt or indecorous language had to be used to make a point. In 1937, representatives of the Pullman Company sat down with leaders of the Brotherhood of Sleeping Car Porters, some twelve years after the union was formed. Well, the company representatives were condescending and coarse. They freely used the terms *nigger* and *darkie* when referring to the porters. After several minutes of these insults, Mr. Randolph, never losing his composure and never mentioning their ill manners, responded with some brief comments and then turned to Milton Webster, the head of the Midwest region of the union, and said: "Mr. Webster, have you anything to say?" Now, Milton Webster was a huge, imposing man, who must have been about six feet five inches tall and weighed 260 pounds. He was a tough, no-nonsense man, known for his outspokenness and his temper. Webster lit into the Pullman executives, calling them every vile name under the sun, questioning their ancestry, and thundering that the porters didn't have to put up with any crap from high-handed white bastards. Just as Webster was hitting his stride, Randolph quietly interrupted, and in his measured and aristocratic tone said, "Mr. Webster, if I may interrupt, I think we ought to proceed with the business at hand." Randolph would never have personally cursed out the Pullman representatives, but by calling on Webster, he knew the company men would get the message, in no uncertain terms, that the porters were not to be patronized. The point made, the meeting proceeded without any more insults from the Pullman representatives. After a series of meetings, the Pullman Company signed a contract with the union, the first time a black union had won an agreement with a white company. Throughout the negotiations, Randolph maintained that air of measured restraint and ultimately won the day.

Randolph also used "deliberate" dignity — that is, dignity for a powerful purpose — in his campaign to end discrimination in the defense industry. Before Pearl Harbor, Randolph had been pressing Franklin Roosevelt to issue an executive order ending segregation in defense plants. When the president hedged, Randolph planned a march on Washington in 1941 to push his demands. At a meeting with Randolph, an exasperated FDR — who was not too eager to desegregate — complained that if a hundred thousand blacks came into Washington, which was a segregated city, there would be no place for them to eat, to sleep, to go to the toilet. After a brief pause, Randolph told the president that if people wanted to come to Washington he was in no position to stop them. Then, in a quiet, even voice, he told the president that if he was really so concerned about where the marchers would eat, sleep, or go to the toilet, he could, by merely picking up a pen, issue an executive order desegregating public accommodations in the entire city. Randolph spoke so quietly and matter-of-factly that it took a moment for the implications of his words to sink in, but when they did, Roosevelt's cigarette-holder nearly fell from his mouth. Randolph had come to talk about desegregating defense plants, and here he was escalating his demands and talking about desegregating public facilities in the whole city. Six months before Pearl Harbor, Roosevelt signed a fair employment practices order which called for an end to discrimination in defense plant jobs. As a result, Randolph called off the march.

But he did not halt his efforts to end discrimination in the armed services, and this led to several clashes with President Truman and other politicians, notably Senator Wayne Morse of Oregon. And it also led to a serious clash between me and Mr. Randolph, the only one in the four decades of our collaboration.

In 1948, Mr. Randolph appointed me executive secretary of the League for Nonviolent Civil Disobedience Against Military Segregation. I had served a three-year sentence in Lewisburg Penitentiary as a conscientious objector during World War II. On 22 March 1948, Randolph and a group of black leaders met with Truman, telling him that unless an executive order were issued barring segregation in the military, blacks would refuse to bear arms in defense of the country and would engage in other acts of civil disobedience. Truman, ever blunt, said he didn't care to hear such talk, and simply adjourned the meeting. By this time, we had some fifty blacks in jail for evading the draft. Undeterred by Truman's rebuff, Randolph went before the Senate Armed Services Committee, testifying that he would personally continue to advise blacks "to refuse to fight as slaves for a democracy they cannot possess and cannot enjoy." This open defiance was too much even for Senator Morse, a liberal and one of Randolph's admirers on the committee. He asked Randolph if he would continue to counsel disobedience and draft evasion even in the event of war. When Randolph said he would because such action was "in the interest of the soul of the country," Morse shot back that such action would be construed by the government as treason. Unflustered, Randolph replied: "We would be willing to absorb the violence, absorb the terrorism, to face the music and to take whatever comes, and we, as a matter of fact, consider that we are more loyal to our country than the people who perpetrate segregation and discrimination upon Negroes because of color or race."

Later that day, Randolph was more emphatic. Speaking to a group of young people at the March on Washington headquarters, he said: "I am prepared to oppose a Jim Crow army until I rot in jail." What made Randolph's position even more courageous was that there were large segments of the black leadership and media that opposed his stand. The influential *Amsterdam News*, the widely read New York paper considered the voice of the black community in America, was against him. Several prominent blacks wrote President Truman assuring him that Randolph spoke only for a small, militant minority of blacks. Even the Urban League had doubts about the wisdom of Randolph's radical stand.

But as was usually the case, Randolph had accurately read the mood of the black people. A poll of young black men in Harlem showed that seventy-one percent favored a civil disobedience campaign against the draft. In July 1948, Randolph led a group of picketers at the Democratic National Convention in Philadelphia. Later that month, President Truman issued Executive Order 9981, calling for an end to military discrimination "as rapidly as possible." After receiving confirmation from presidential advisors that the order did indeed ban segregation, Randolph called off the civil disobedience campaign and moved to disband the League for Nonviolent Civil Disobedience.

Being young and impetuous at the time, I argued that dissolving the League would be unfair to those blacks who were still in jail for refusing to serve in the armed forces. Randolph, always a man of great honor, would not be swayed, noting that he had given his solemn word to the president of the United States. He had demanded an executive order, and that demand had been met. Unsatisfied with that answer, a number of "Young Turks" and I decided to outflank Mr. Randolph. He had asked me to call a press conference for four o'clock on 17 August 1948 in order to announce the dissolution of the League. Well, we called a press conference of our own for ten o'clock that morning, during which we denounced Randolph as an Uncle Tom, a sellout, a reactionary, and an old fogey out of touch with the times. Of course, we got all the headlines. For months we continued to operate the League, sending out correspondence and continuing to embarrass Mr. Randolph. Finally, Randolph was forced to issue a statement. Always a man of great tact and patience, he did not blast us for our impertinence. He merely said that the League had been co-opted by a pacifist element that, while useful to keep the movement nonviolent, now had its own agenda.

Such was Randolph's stature that the League lost all influence and resources quickly dried up. It finally collapsed in November 1948. Guilt-ridden and ashamed, and sure that Randolph would never forgive me for my treachery, I avoided him for two whole years. I was convinced that even a man of such understanding, dignity, and forbearance would never forget being stabbed in the back by trusted confidants and friends. When I finally mustered the courage to go see him, I went to his modest union office on 125th Street, the very place I had first met him some ten years earlier, expecting to be chastised for my recklessness. As I was ushered in, there he was, distinguished and dapper as ever, with arms outstretched, waiting to greet me, the way he had done a decade ago. Motioning me to sit down with that same sweep of his arm, he looked at me, and in a calm, even voice said: "Bayard, where have you been? You know that I have needed you." I was moved and overwhelmed. For the rest of our long friendship, he never, ever mentioned what I had done to him.

Mr. Randolph's crowning achievement, the 1963 March on Washington, which led to a confrontation with President Kennedy, also included a dramatic and trying episode that threatened my personal reputation and the march itself. Again, Randolph's dignity and nerve saved my career and what was to become a watershed event of the civil rights movement.

When Randolph asked me to organize the march, he envisioned it as a march for jobs and freedom. By now a member of the AFL-CIO Executive Council (the first black to hold this position), Randolph understood that the upcoming phase of the civil rights movement would involve economic justice. In planning the march, Randolph did not consult with the other black leaders until all the mechanisms were in place, presenting them with a fait accompli they would find hard to refuse. When final preparations were being made, a nervous President Kennedy, who had been working to get civil rights legislation passed in Congress, called a meeting of a number of top black leaders on 22 June 1963. The president voiced his concern about possible violence and the fact that some congressmen might not vote for the legislation if they felt pressured by a mass demonstration in the nation's capital. His position was that one simply could not bully Congress. After comments from other black leaders, Randolph took the floor, speaking with, as Arthur Schlesinger would later recall, "the quiet dignity which touched Kennedy as it had touched Roosevelt before him." Noting the inevitability of the march, Randolph said: "Mr. President, the Negroes are already in the streets. It is very likely impossible to get them off. If they are bound to be in the streets in any case, is it not better that they be led by organizations dedicated to civil rights and disciplined by struggle rather than to leave them to other leaders who care neither about civil rights nor nonviolence?"

With those words, Randolph not only convinced Kennedy that the march was unstoppable, but got him to endorse it as well.

But just as plans were being made final, a serious crisis arose that would test Randolph's trust in me and all his skills as a leader. Six weeks before the march, Senator Strom Thurmond stood before the Senate and for over three-quarters of an hour attacked me as the organizer of the march in an effort to disrupt and divide the black leadership. He accused me of being a draft-dodger, a Communist, and a homosexual. The papers jumped all over the story. It made the front page of the *New York Times*, and it was plastered in papers around the country. By this time, the march had gained international attention. As expected, Senator Thurmond's accusations caused pandemonium among the black leadership. Roy Wilkins had predicted that if I were made chief organizer of the march these charges would be made.

Randolph quickly called the black leaders together, and there was a fierce debate over my future role. He said that the purpose of Thurmond's remarks was to destroy the march, and that the purpose of the meeting was to make certain that he did not succeed. He then said he had already prepared a statement which he wanted all the leaders of the march to sign, adding that he had called a press conference for the next day at which he would read the statement and tell the media that all the leaders had agreed to it. The statement read: "We have absolute confidence in Bayard Rustin's ability and character, and he will continue to organize the march, which we know will be a great success." Many of the leaders expressed concern that the press would hound them for further comments, to which Mr. Randolph said that the only way to put an end to the controversy was for all of them to repeat the simple statement he had just read.

The next morning, Mr. Randolph met the press alone. It was the biggest press conference to date dealing with the march. There must have been fifty people there from newspapers and radio and television stations around the country. For ten minutes after he read the statement, the press tried to goad Mr. Randolph to say more. They badgered him with questions. With his customary self-control and calm, Randolph simply repeated the one-line statement. He said it so quietly that the press corps had to lean in to hear him. And the reporters, who had been incessantly pumping Randolph for more information, recognized the inner strength of this dignified man and burst into spontaneous applause. It was an unbelievable moment. And six weeks later, on 28 August, over 250,000 people gathered in Washington for the largest demonstration ever held in the capital. Only a person of Mr. Randolph's impeccable character and integrity could have pulled the whole thing out of the fire.

The way Mr. Randolph decisively handled the crisis that arose before the march taught me lessons that would later help me act quickly to protect his dignity. After the March on Selma in 1965, during which he walked several grueling miles in the blazing sun, Mr. Randolph, who was already over seventy and suffered from a serious heart condition, passed out at the train station. Almost immediately, press photographers rushed over, trying to get a picture of the stricken warrior lying on the ground. I quickly got together a group of tough, brawny associates, and we formed a human wall to keep the photographers away. At one point, in the heat of the moment, I unfortunately snatched a camera from someone who had taken a picture and ripped the film out. To this day I regret losing my temper. My associates and I surrounded the Chief until I managed to get Dick Gregory's plane to fly Mr. Randolph to New York and get him to a hospital. Later, a reporter came up to me and complained that the press had to make a living, and the fact that Mr. Randolph had collapsed after the march was news. I recall saying to the man: "It will be over my dead body that anyone ever sees a man of Mr. Randolph's dignity lying helpless on the ground." For over four decades Phil Randolph, with moral fortitude and nobility, had won victories that were the key stepping-stones to racial and economic equality for blacks. He had become a symbol of strength and progress. At that moment in Selma, a critical juncture for the civil rights movement he helped launch, I knew I could not allow any impression, any suggestion to emerge, even for a moment, that our gentle warrior was vanquished.

Seeking Out Christina Stead

However limited my memoir of Christina Stead must be, I should like to record it. I met her only twice, but because she was the one writer I was ever brash enough to set out to find, her image remains with me: an older writer, whose reverberations I can recall in a doubled way, now that I can see her from two places in time, separated by some thirty years.

In 1952 Little, Brown and Company published *The People with the Dogs*, listed as Stead's ninth book. Their editor John Woodburn, who had recently published my first stories, sent me a copy. I had previously read and marveled at Stead's *The Man Who Loved Children*—as had several other writers then unknown to me, among them Stanley Burnshaw, Elizabeth Hardwick and Robert Lowell, and Randall Jarrell. I had read enough of her work (probably *Letty Fox, Her Luck*, and *House of All Nations*) to feel that here was a writer of powerful originality whose books migrated from publisher to publisher even more rapidly than those of most literary writers (five different houses being responsible for the nine American editions I now own)—and that this might be part of the reason she was so little known here.

As yet I had never written a professional piece of criticism, but it seemed to me that someone ought to bring Stead to more notice. Authoritative or not, I must try. Then, talking about her work with Randall Jarrell after a lecture of his at Barnard, I learned that Elizabeth Hardwick intended to write just such a piece. This relieved me of the responsibility. Yet I might still try to look up Stead on a projected trip to London. Had she been merely a writer I admired, I'd have been shy of doing so. But she was also a mystery.

Once settled in London, I went to Foyle's to buy books, among them those by Stead not yet published in the United States. A glance showed that she had had as many different publishers in England as with us. On impulse I telephoned her most recent one—Peter Davies?—gave my British publishers as reference and was ceded an address to write to, which I did. The

British mails being what they then were, I had her answering note the next day. We arranged to meet and dine at the Arts Theatre Club, then the liveliest of its kind, where a visitor like me could have a temporary membership for a small sum. Over the phone she repeated what her note had told me: "Why, I read your stories when we were at The Hague."

That awed me. My one book had been reviewed abroad but I had as yet no real sense of being read there, and no "writer" façade — that is, the inevitable savvy generated by years of having similar things said to one in professional chitchat, and even the same encounters, more or less. It seemed to me that Christina Stead must really keep up with literature, and this pointed to the dizzy possibility that I myself might belong there. In New York I had met a few writers, among them William Maxwell at the *New Yorker*, and Louis Auchincloss, Norman Mailer, and William Styron, at Tina and Vance Bourjaily's parties. The well-known women of the day — Katherine Anne Porter, Jean Stafford, Kay Boyle — inhabited other bohemias. As a woman living a family life upriver, I was something of an anomaly at any. Yet, going to meet Stead it never occurred to me that she was the first woman writer of stature I would be meeting or that we were meeting as two "woman writers." I doubt that this last occurred to her either. It was a time when writers were not that segregated. We met as workers interested in each other's work — I merely in possession as yet of much more to go on than she.

The Arts' patrons were of two kinds. Half were people "in the profession," including a stream of young actresses intent on looking gorgeous and men interested in meeting them. Half were audience regulars of the solid London kind, the women not the fluffy matinée sort one might see on a New York Wednesday afternoon but country matrons in town for the day — and for a play.

The woman who came toward me might have been one of those, amply bosomed in her tan twin-sweater set, big-boned rather than fat, a good strong face. I could see her in a suburban garden; I could see her almost anywhere. As we know from her work, almost anywhere was where she felt herself able to be. Her actual radii were not enormous — London, Paris, New York, the Eastern Shore of Maryland and nearby Bucks County, plus her native Australia. But once in that milieu she loved, of funky houses not quite fallen from grace, endlessly slipper-easy kitchen-table conversations, and ideas siphoning like fungi through what a minute ago was a domestic scene, she could bring you the soul and smell of wherever she chose.

I thought of this as she told me that she and her husband had lately returned from Germany—East Germany, she said, not West—with a keen glance. More from her work than from the literary gossip I was so little privy to, I knew that she must belong to that group of fellow travelers in the arts during the 1930s whose critics had dubbed them "pink tea Communists." At home I had had some acquaintance with a local group who were younger inheritors of a Party line in which mateyness, equated with loyalty, had appeared to me to outweigh logic. How it might have happened that Stead and her husband had gone to the East by choice—or to Germany in general, still anathema to me because of the Holocaust—did give me pause. Yet in talking with her, although I no longer recall her precise words, or mine, I remember feeling that this woman made her own choices within a frame she understood and approved.

She did ask me whether I was "political." I told her that on very minor occasions I had tried, but that group-thinking bothered me. Asked what kind of action I had tried, I told her that after the birth of my second child, I had lived in Grosse Pointe Park, a plush suburb of Detroit; as an antidote I had interviewed Detroit candidates for city office (garbage division) for the League of Women Voters, and later had worked as a volunteer in a presidential campaign with the United Electrical Workers Union (actually the Briggs Local, of whose notoriety I had been unaware). She smiled at my description of "the Pointe," of which she apparently knew, but I felt she thought me a political innocent. I in turn thought that she, though far more seasoned in a political companionship based partly on working-class experience and partly on upper-echelon theory, would in the end keep her innocence through her books.

I told her how remarkable I knew her evocation of Maryland's Eastern Shore to be (in *The Man Who Loved Children*), since I had lived in nearby Delaware. I saw that she regarded my obvious love of London as somewhat misguided—as an Australian well might, and also as might a writer who had been greeted with dazzling reviews in 1934 (for *The Salzburg Tales*) but was now, twenty years later, comparatively unknown. (Not too much later, asking C. P. Snow about her—who, with his wife Pamela Hansford Johnson, kept as abreast of the literary world as any there—I would be shocked to learn that they had never heard of her.)

Before we went in to dinner we were joined briefly by her husband William Blake, who had wished to meet me but refused my invitation to stay on. I knew he had changed his name from Blech (though not why he had chosen that glorious patronymic), that he had written a novel about our Civil War called *The Copperheads*, and — he confirmed, somewhat vaguely — that he had worked for financial institutions of some sort. His manner was courtly, even elaborate — what we Americans used to call "European" or even "boulevardier." It was clear that they had agreed between them that he was not to stay on. I had a strong impression that they were indeed a very close couple, whose pattern was to "gypsy" together around the world — a word she herself had used. Two-against-the-world might even be the attitude, quixotic if not revolutionary. She, I was sure, was a writer above all — and would wish me to judge her by her books, above all.

At dinner, what I recall best is that we were astonishingly unliterary, yet comfortable. If we talked about "books," I cannot remember it. I must have told her in some way or other that I wished to do anything she thought useful to promote her work in the United States. Nor do I recall how and when we exchanged notes later, at which time I would introduce her by letter to the agent Cyrilly Abels, under whose aegis a modest Stead renaissance was begun. (Her 1976 book, *Miss Herbert [The Suburban Wife]*, is dedicated to Abels.)

Over the years I had an occasional note from her, but the only letter I can locate now is the one I append. In 1960, when I taught *The Man Who Loved Children* in a graduate seminar, one of the class, Eldon Branda, who was later to teach at the University of Texas at Austin, became devoted to that novel and wrote a play based on it — and some correspondence ensued because of that.

It must have been sometime during the 1960s that Stead and Blake returned briefly to New York (possibly for a book publication) and invited my husband and me to a party that was given for her. It was a "brownstone" party, recognizably of an era; Philip Van Doren Stern may have been the host. Other names reverberated; Donald Ogden Stewart was one, and others whose very habit of using three sonorous names evoked their period. Stead, handsome in a long dress and taller than I remembered, was the happy center of her old crowd. The crowd itself, older now, and roughly treated by history, might look frowsty to younger eyes, and unduly acerb — a bohemia that knew itself for a backwater now. Maybe all bohemias ended like this — slapping each other's backs and spirits on a jaunty Sunday afternoon? Or was this crowd, in its mix of inherited money, applied radicalism, and determinedly international know-how, slightly adolescent even in age?

I could picture a younger Stead in their midst, gawky with talent, their red-cheeked colonial. Her face, bent now toward theirs in nostalgic pleasure, seemed the most vigorous, and planed by broader sympathies; she was deservedly their star. Work must have kept it so, through all the vicissitudes of money. I recalled a prefatory note to *Letty Fox*—"This is a work of fiction. The persons and events other than political are imaginary. The language and opinions are those of a type of middleclass New York office worker. The jokes and stories in Chapter XXVIII are not original but are taken from conversations heard in midtown Manhattan"—and wondered how many accessory jobs she might have held during the Depression years, or thereafter. And even among these linked intimacies, and floating on her "conversations," she was clearly the observer still.

In 1967 or thereabouts, I reviewed *The Puzzleheaded Girl* for *Life* magazine and sent her the review, which never was published because it had been bumped by a book they considered more timely. Later she sent me one or two magazine tributes to her work which she thought I might like to see. Though she did not complain and was cheered by her American publication, this was surely the gesture of a writer who must see her lifework as too little appreciated for the scope she must have known it had. During those years Blake became blind; it determined their life. I believe it was after his death that she returned to Australia, later sending me clips to show she now had some renown there also.

When she was made an honorary member of the American Academy and Institute of Arts and Letters I wrote asking whether she could come for the ceremony. I was told that she was unable, and heard no more, except for a letter from her brother after her death.

Over the years I had brooded over aspects of her work that might have prevented its wider acceptance, notably that verbosity mentioned in a review of her first book, *The Salzburg Tales*—"Her verbosity is that of passion and genius" (Sir John Squire, *Daily Telegraph*). On the same jacket Rebecca West says: "Delightful miscellany . . . the work of a strong, idiosyncratic talent." That book, which I read long after the later books, had to me too many elaborate derivations, but is certainly as West says. I no longer have my copy of *The Beauty and the Furies*, listed in the American editions of her works as her third, but I recall that while every page had its brilliance, the total outpour did seem at times indigestible. *Dark Places of the Heart*, on the other hand, published abroad as *Cotter's England*, is transacted in household conversations, alternating with narrative in a tone so close to the down-to-earth characters and their concrete lives that it seems all but narrated by them. Stead knew trade-unionist life in all its fluid blend of working-class saltiness, socialist ethic, and rainbow ideals. Nor is Stead ever boring or instructive, in the way of some proletarian novelists of the era — and that world is only one of her worlds. In her work, people and their lives took precedence, and she had a gift for putting talk and life-story together. Her exploration of the nonsexual relationships between women, one that well precedes Doris Lessing's *The Golden Notebook*, may have gone unnoticed, perhaps because it is performed without partisan-ship. She has the tolerant overview that all great writers have; everybody gets a fair shake.

Yet this can mitigate against "story" in a novel — even to those who do not demand too formal a path of progression, yet require a provided sense of its moving on. On the farther side there are those novels which we excuse as poems of action rather than accounts reasonably rendered. Stead's longer books fall somewhere in between. One follows the people and the talk. Simple as the single sentence may be, their tumbled abundance creates a style. Actions follow one another in a whirlpool of knowledge and allusion — she knows so much. Or one wallows in the locale. There Stead's sense of place — of any place — is as geographic as Balzac's and as descrip-tive, often with a comic sensuousness in which the very lay of the land con-tributes to the sardonic voice in which a novel sometimes unfolds.

In *The Man Who Loved Children* all this unites. In a fundamental picture of a province, of its clans and economy, its placement in historical time and its neighborly allegiances, we are borne along on an astonishingly "native" command of its very backchat, flora, and kitchen lore. And this time it is the central character who is verbose, but to an evil degree. Verbosity itself connects psychologically with motive, to become "story." The exaggeration of the language impulse rests not with author but with Sam Pollit, which is why it succeeds. Meanwhile, the way Stead sees women — as wildly powerful behind the scenes but titularly subjects of the men and therefore always imbalanced in their emotions toward each other as well — works its own tragedy.

What has all this to do with meeting an author in the flesh? Little or much, depending on whether one sees a writer as somehow embodied in the work one knows, or not — a quarrel that will never be answered. At the Arts Theatre Club, Stead to my outward eye was an older writer drawing out a younger one with grace and perhaps a certain wearied experience.

What was said, however peripheral, echoed backward into her books. When I admired England I saw the tucked-in colonial smile of the author of *For Love Alone*, that story of a gifted émigré, which begins with a magnificent one-page paean to Australia called "Sea People," prelude to a novel whose first half is titled "The Island Continent," and the second, "Port of Registry: London." Where I felt my own innocences of the political or bohemian world, or the bourse, it was in part because in each of those arenas I could be confronted by one or more of her books. Yet the writer sitting across from me almost regally alone, or in that brief connubial scene where I caught two sharp, collusive minds focused on me, casts a penumbra on which I can still reminisce. What made her choose worlds so nimbly and adroitly, which yet in book after book turn out to resemble one another deep down?

During the moments when Blake was there I had a sense of a coupledom more than close — irremediable in its way of life. To two-against-the-world, would each successive reality, however engorged, be doctrinaire and temporary? The United States had quite apparently been important to them both, on terms I could only surmise. For him, possibly as a country to reject. For her, as a greater colonial world to engage in with all her talents, describe compellingly, and leave — only to return there with that nostalgic perspective which could now impute what had been important, as at that party where I watched her bloom and turn almost young.

Where two people are the family frame, friendships can become that much more important, and friendship in many inflections was often her theme. Had the relative formlessness of their traveling, reacting to necessity or to allegiances, made for a Canterbury Tale objectivity in which the permanencies became scenery and talk? Did that itinerant life have its counterpart in novels sometimes formless in toto, but always sitting down to an intensely framed room?

When Blake left, her face sombered; they were jauntier together. As a writer she would have had humiliations I did not then suspect. They may also have lived often on the financial edge. I had an idea that Blake's knowledge of the banking world may have been crucial to her work — notably in *The House of All Nations*, which for all its four-page cast of characters has a scatty shallowness unusual in her prose.

I remember her as both open and silent — as I now know writers so often are. Experience sat on her somewhat acidulously, an old eagle on her shoulder. Yet she had wanted to meet a new person — and in an almost kindly fashion, had set the tone. We were not there to be brilliant together. Yet I didn't feel unsatisfied with this writer I had sought out. She had an intimate majesty.

One daren't have evidential conversations with the dead. Yet one has them. What would she have said to William Blake when they rejoined each other in whatever was their perching-place? Perhaps: "She too is a candidate."

Here is the letter I have:

158 Adelaide Road, N.W.3
31st August, 1956

Dear Miss Calisher:

Thanks very much for your kind letter. I should be delighted to see you, at your convenience. Perhaps you would be kind enough to telephone me?

I was reading a very interesting story of yours the other day, THE HOLLOW BOY, (Harper's October, '52) about Werner Houser. This appealed to me, I knew this kind of background in New York — well, partly, at least I knew that kind of boy, grown up. It was a wonderful picture, especially the tight pale little mother making strudel. A friend of mine had a mother who made strudel and he helped in that way — but it certainly wasn't Werner. . . . I also read your interesting CHRISTMAS CARILLON (in Harper's 1953); and when we were in The Hague, a year or two ago, I took all the short story and poetry books out of the American Library. One of them was your book of short stories. (You may wonder, by the way at my recently reading those old Harper's. We have been gipsying — far too much and I have been out of contact. My husband recently picked up a lot of old Harper's that the Am. Library had in duplicate and so on.)

I heard that John Woodburn died some time ago. I liked him, he was original and a kindhearted chap.

Kind regards,
Yours sincerely,

(Mrs. W. J. Blake)   Christina Stead

On the left-hand margin of the letter, written upward from the bottom, in Stead's handwriting is:

My husband is an American writer.

HARRY LEVIN

Jean Renoir

It is to a series of other encounters that I owe my chance acquaintance with Jean Renoir. During the 1940s he had been exiled by the war from Europe to Hollywood. The most congenial of men in a not altogether congenial situation, he had there encountered an exile from Broadway, Clifford Odets. Between the film director of the Popular Front and the leading playwright of the Group Theatre, an ideological affinity had developed into a close friendship. When Odets died in 1963, Renoir would present a bronze mask of his face to the Harvard Theatre Collection — and when Renoir was told that the library already possessed a death mask of Walt Whitman, he wrote back to tell me how pleased Clifford would have been at finding himself enshrined along with his literary hero. But I am getting ahead of my encounter. Its vital link was Jean's son, Alain Renoir, who had joined his father in this country and was applying in 1949 to Harvard's Ph.D. program in Comparative Literature. After his arduous service in both the French and the American armies, his undergraduate record looked rather casual. But his letter of application was quite impressive, and it was persuasively reinforced by a personal letter of recommendation from Odets, with whom I had been very slightly acquainted. This good opinion turned out to have been well justified. Alain has long been a professor of English and a respected medieval scholar in the University of California at Berkeley.

As it would happen, in 1952–1953 I was sent to France as an exchange professor from Harvard to the Sorbonne. By a mere coincidence, through arrangements made for us by other French acquaintances, our family happened to spend the preceding summer in the old Provençal hill town of Cagnes-sur-Mer. From our little terrace, just below the chateau, we could look down upon the Mediterranean in one direction and up toward the Maritime Alps in another. Straight across a valley of vineyards and orange tile rooftops, we could catch a glimpse of Les Collettes, the hillside estate where the great Impressionist had lived and worked in the mellowness of his last years. A museum today, the house was then still occupied by Claude ("Coco"), the youngest of the artist's three sons. (Pierre Renoir, the eldest, had become a well-known actor; typically, Jean came in between his two brothers.) Claude Renoir, kindly apprised of our local sojourn by his American nephew, graciously invited us to tea, did the honors of the paternal studio, and showed us through those immortal groves of twisted olive trees. Later on, in Paris, we would meet other living Renoirs. One of them, intermarried with the Cézannes, conducted an Impressionistic chocolate shop in the Faubourg Saint-Honoré. Alain's cousin, the lively and learned Edmond Renoir, who had recently retired from teaching English at a lycée, proved extremely helpful in showing me what to expect from my students and in putting me in touch with several university colleagues.

Jean Renoir himself had meanwhile been in Italy, as we were to learn, making his colorful film with Anna Magnani, *Le Carrosse d'or*. Soon after his return he introduced himself, and the mode of introduction was characteristic both for him and for Paris: a short handwritten note on pale bluish paper, transmitted by pneumatic tube from the Champs Elysées to the Rive Gauche. Needless to say, it has been saved and prized, particularly for the overwhelming modesty of its opening statement: *"Monsieur, je suis le père de votre ancien élève. . . ."* Having grown up as the son of a famous man, clearly he preferred to bask in Alain's light rather than to interpose his own shadow. We happily accepted his invitation, and were even happier after an elegant dinner together and an evening's buoyant conversation with him and with his Brazilian wife and assistant, the beautiful and intelligent Dido Freire. He was on the verge of sixty at the time; but it was not difficult to reconcile his appearance with the boy Auguste Renoir had so memorably painted as an irresistible Pierrot, among many other guises, and as a youthful huntsman in a portrait that had accompanied him to California. For such purposes of portraiture, his golden-reddish hair had not been cut short until he had attained the age of six, and this was his one grudge against his father. Sometimes, he said, he would have preferred to be bald, and now at last he seemed to be approaching that fulfillment.

He had retained from childhood the round-faced rosiness that made him so much his mother's son. She had been his father's ideal model, and her full-bodied femininity must have contrasted strikingly with her husband's angular figure and aquiline features. Yet it was from his father that Jean inherited a lifelong commitment to the interpretation and celebration of womanhood. The individual — of course a woman — who influenced him most, as he often attested, was Gabrielle Renard. A cousin of his mother from rural Burgundy, she had joined the household at his birth, when she was sixteen, serving as his nursemaid and modeling for his father. Jean, born into the Belle Epoque at Montmartre, would recall those formative occasions when she had taken him to see Guignol at the puppet show or to hear the *chanteuses* at a *café-concert*. While he was posing, she had kept him from restlessness by reading aloud from Andersen's fairy tales; and it would be one of these that inspired his experimental film *La Petite Marchande d'allumettes*, featuring the painter's last model, Catherine Hessling, who became Jean's first wife. There would be an element of the fairy tale throughout his work as a cinematic storyteller (*"raconteur d'histoires"*). But fantasy was leavened by naturalism, and some of his scenarios would be based upon fiction by Zola, Maupassant, and Flaubert. War might be the grandest of illusions, to instance his best-known film; but art was a process of demystification, to echo a favorite word.

His unique relationship with Auguste Renoir emerges, not only from his volume of filial reminiscence, but in his autobiographical book about his films. It crystallized at Cagnes after Madame Renoir's death, when Jean — home from World War I severely wounded — had to assume responsibility for the *modus vivendi* of the increasingly crippled artist. True to their artisan heritage from Limoges, his own artistic training had also begun with ceramics. This was a germane apprenticeship for the new medium toward which he was gravitating, since the cinema was a primarily visual craft. However, with the development of sound, it became secondarily verbal; and with his ear for speech, his remarkable flair for spoken dialogue, he would do as much as anyone to weather the ensuing crisis and shape the talking film. At times he met with controversies that must have made him feel as if he were reliving the pioneer stages of his father's career. The qualities shared in abundance by both of them — independence, warmth, sincerity — shine through the technical differences between their respective media. Something like a laying on of hands is prefigured by a relic of primitive film, cranked out by Gaumont cameramen for Jean at Les Collettes. There we may jerkily witness the aged painter being pushed in his wheelchair to his studio or through his orchards, his brushes swathed to his arthritic hands, his palette mixed for him by his son, and painting

La Boulangère (actually his cook) or chatting with his friend and dealer, Ambroise Vollard.

That was a home movie for posterity, not merely a documentary for students of art history but a record in the annals of civilization. Consequently, there is now a print of it in the Library of Congress, presented by Jean Renoir in 1957. At the same time, with congenital generosity, he offered a copy to Harvard. Living up to its puritanical origins, the Harvard Corporation was not interested. As his emissary, I was informed that the university had not yet framed a policy in this underdeveloped area and would therefore be reluctant to set a precedent by any unwary acceptance. Fortunately McGeorge Bundy, then Dean of the Faculty, managed to persuade the governing body that educational values were not being jeopardized. Thus the existence of film as a means of expression was belatedly and grudgingly, but officially, recognized. Harvard has since been trying hard, with programs and professorships and archives, to make up for its stuffy neglect of cinematography. It may have rounded a corner in 1965, when Jean Renoir delivered our annual public lecture on the drama. This has been a distinguished series inaugurated by T. S. Eliot, in which some of us were hoping to see the cinema represented, and we were exceptionally fortunate in being able to call upon so articulate and authoritative a spokesman. Accordingly, though we had him in mind from the outset, we would wait until he was free to come; and he, on his part, took the assignment very seriously. Our one retrospective regret is that his address went unrecorded.

I am not sure that he had had any previous experience as a lecturer in English, though he would soon be holding forth successfully as a visiting Regents' Professor at Berkeley. Certainly he could draw upon his talents as a conversationalist and his skills as an *improvisatore*. Yet, though he and Dido were by no means less warm than usual, when my wife and I greeted them at the airport and lunched with them at the Faculty Club, he seemed uncharacteristically abstracted and even a little nervous. He was anxious to spend the two hours between lunch and the lecture in their quarters at the university guest house, quietly gathering his thoughts. When we picked them up again, he had fortified himself — not with a typescript or a sheaf of notes, but with a single card, on which he seemed to have written no more than two or three words. I could observe this because, when we arrived at the college theater, it was so packed that the chairman, after

introducing the speaker, could not slip down into the auditorium, but had
to sit back and watch the rows of interested faces from the stage. I wished
that I could eavesdrop over his shoulder, and I still tingle with unallayed
curiosity as to the magic formula or gnomic wisdom spelled out in that suc-
cinct notation. Obviously, we must have heard it at some point; but then,
we went on to hear so much. He talked for nearly an hour and a half, and
might well have kept his audience enthralled for an additional hour.

Since the broad title he chose was "Considerations on Film-Making," he
had many further opportunities to discourse upon that subject, through
interviews and articles and books which more luckily survive. The
irreplaceable aspect of this particular occasion was the oral spell he exer-
cised through his complete control of its human dimensions. Ivy League
students are quick to shrug off whatever they perceive as sentimentality,
to raise their eyebrows at overt expressions of love for one's fellow men.
(Was that the message on the little card? Jean would hardly have needed
to write it down.) But as an accomplished master of his demanding craft,
he held the respect and admiration of his hearers. Most of them had seen
La Grande Illusion, where the French aviators imprisoned in a German for-
tress so concretely embodied the object-lesson of "la réunion des hommes,"
of fraternity under stress, of camaraderie across battle lines and class
conflicts. He spoke with special affection of Erich von Stroheim, who as
the austere Prussian commandant had contributed much of his own to the
part, and of Jean Gabin, who as a warm-hearted workingman wore the
pilot's uniform that Jean Renoir had cast off when he became a pacifist after
World War I. If I could not read his jotting, I could remember the saying
of another wise Frenchman, Pascal: "La vraie éloquence se moque de l'éloquence." Such eloquent plainspeaking must have formed an effective and
reductive contrast to the more academic effusions from our daily lecture
platforms.

Communication was never unilateral for Jean Renoir, and the impact of
his lecture was registered through excited feedback at a reception afterward
in the clubhouse of the student literary society. It deeply gratified him that
a nearby cinema was currently reviving La Règle du jeu, and that his young
American auditors were so eager to talk with him about it. That problematic masterpiece is now accorded classical status; its hysterical house-
party in a proud chateau has been recognized as a kind of allegory for the
Europe of 1939, when its first presentation was badly cut and critically

assaulted. In it the author-director, who liked to play incidental parts in his pictures, for once assumed a central role. He was cast in character as Octave, the music critic who wanted to be a conductor, no romantic hero but a sympathetic confidant, the sole person in that assemblage who is not playing his own game, though amiably prancing through the masquerade scene in the costume of a dancing bear. The high point of those Cambridge discussions, as Jean Renoir recollected them in *Les Films de ma vie*, was his realization that *La Règle du jeu* was becoming widely appreciated at last. At the Fogg Museum he was also shown some of his father's sketches of Gabrielle. Juxtaposed to these blooming nudes — through a request from our curators and the courtesy of Alain — was the recent photograph of a handsome, dignified, octogenarian lady: Gabrielle (Mrs. Conrad Slade) in California, widow of an American painter and neighbor of her former nursling.

His links with Harvard were strengthened when he gave three of his original scripts to its Theatre Collection, among them a working version — heavily revised and annotated — of *La Grande Illusion*. He went so far as to outline another script (*Christine*), never filmed but posthumously published, wherein one of the characters has prepared himself for a sequence of misadventures by studying Shakespeare at Harvard. Though we talked about and hoped for another visit, it never materialized. Yet, on my occasional visits to Los Angeles, we enjoyed a few more brief reunions: at his home in Beverly Hills (a transatlantic Les Collettes, authenticated by relics in paint and clay) or my brother's house across another valley. And on one festive evening together in San Francisco, we saw a repertory company do better than New York had done with a play by his friend Odets. Except for the sprightly television vaudeville *Le Petit Théâtre de Jean Renoir*, he turned out no more films during the final decade of his life. Rather, he turned increasingly into the man of letters that, to a large extent, he had always been. Readers were taken by surprise when, at seventy-two, he produced a romantic — indeed a highly erotic — novel, shot through with vivid wartime memories, *Les Cahiers du Capitaine Georges*. It should not be surprising that his printed scripts are readable as novels. As a scenario writer, he laid the ground for his integral authority as a director.

In a word, he set the example and formulated the concept of the *auteur*. His influence as such has been seminal for the next generation of directors, and he in turn would welcome and applaud their Nouvelle Vague. The "author," by his professional definition, was not so much an omnipotent creator as a sensitive midwife. In so collective an enterprise as the film, it was his principal function to absorb rather than impose, to bring out the actors and all the others involved, and help them to interact. "The only way to express his personality," Renoir himself has stated, "is to assist his collaborators in expressing theirs." Many of those who collaborated with him, notably the scene designer Eugène Lourié, have testified that they were treated as creative partners, jointly participating in the struggles and satisfactions of authorship. Just as Auguste's servants had posed for him, so Jean's technicians now and then were called upon to act — it was all in the extended family. But his familial outlook was worldwide. He was fond of quoting from Kipling's jungle-boy Mowgli: "We are of the same blood, you and I." In The River he dramatized that attitude by bringing East and West together on Mowgli's own terrain. Citizen of two countries, he was devoted to and critical of both; his feeling for humane relations freely transcended the constrictions of nationalism. One could not have accidentally crossed his far-flung path without feeling some touch of the insights and sympathies that characterize his monumental work.

Three Passions of
Paul Hindemith

In 1949, while yet a boy-soldier and deciding what to do with my musical life, I read an article in a jazz magazine in which Charlie Parker, the legendary alto saxophonist and composer, was interviewed. The question was put to him: "Bird, if you could use your time any way you wanted to, what would you do?" Parker answered: "I would go to New Haven to Yale, where there is a little German cat teaching composition, and I would sit at his feet and learn some music." That was Paul Hindemith.

I was seventeen years old then. I had run away from home at fourteen to enlist, and had spent most of my three-and-a-half-year army stint teaching myself to play the French horn and the bass viol. I had picked up enough of the required skills at my two instruments to begin thinking of getting myself educated beyond the nighttime tutoring given me by generous officers and their wives at Lockbourne Air Base in Ohio. I had a burning interest in jazz music and had earned enough money by playing around the watering holes at Lockbourne and in Columbus to pay for a college education with the help of the GI Bill.

Charlie Parker's answer settled the question of what to do next. If sitting at the feet of Paul Hindemith was good enough for Charlie Parker, it was good enough for me, so I applied to Yale's School of Music and was accepted.

Hindemith was clearly the king of the musical mountain at Yale, and I was not disappointed to learn that only by working my way up through the more elementary music courses taught by others would I be admitted to a Hindemith class. In the meantime, I sought to find out just who Paul Hindemith really was. Why had the little German cat's music appealed so much to Charlie Parker? What had Hindemith's life been before New Haven?

Hitler had declared Hindemith's music decadent and banned its performance in Germany. Hindemith had moved to Switzerland, found work in Turkey, and later emigrated to America, settling at Yale in 1940. He was a thundering paradox. I was astounded to learn that he'd spent no more time in school than I had. The precocious boy, Paul, had not bothered to show up much for school back in his native Germany, being too busy teaching himself. He taught himself so well, in fact, and he played the violin so brilliantly that, much to the envy of other boys his age, his truancy went unnoticed — or worse, unpunished — by the authorities. To support himself, he had played the drums in jazz bands and written music for films, mechanical instruments, and plays produced by both professionals and schoolchildren.

So the greatest contradiction in that whole complicated life story for me was that this most learned and distinguished of professors — one who had taught medieval Latin and mathematics at the Hochschule in Berlin, revamped the entire system of music education in Turkey, shuttled between the lecture halls of Yale and Harvard — had all his life so energetically avoided formal schooling. Here was a man who took his education strictly à la carte.

After two years, the day arrived for my first Hindemith class, History of the Theory of Music. At the first class meeting, I had to elbow my way through the packed lecture hall to a seat. I didn't know what to expect. I hoped Hindemith might want to talk about modern chords or some subject close to "new" ideas in music. But I challenged myself to take my professor as I found him. After all, the great Charlie Parker wanted to be where I was.

Hindemith was a small man who exuded self-assurance. His intense, piercing eyes, though, reflected strength rather than arrogance or snobbery. He was just then returning to Yale from a year at Harvard, where he'd been the resident Norton Lecturer and had written his much-celebrated book, *A Composer's World*.

His first lecture in History of the Theory of Music confused me and put me off. I kept asking myself as he talked why he was so hung up on the past. He talked about Boethius, Pythagoras, the "music of the spheres," and the ancient Greek notion that all things are number or explainable by number. "The quadrivium," he said, "those four subjects whose concerns are 'measure' — geometry, astronomy, mathematics, and music — formed the core of an educated person's learning in better times." Why better times?

He then filled the blackboard with numbers representing ratios of vibrating frequencies that make up musical tones and the resulting harmony of tones sounding together. Directing his steady gaze at us and rubbing his hands, he said, "The list of great scientists and philosophers through the ages who have *also* written on music theory is long and impressive. They include Ptolemy, Euclid, Descartes, and, of course, Johannes Kepler. Johannes Kepler, an astronomer driven by a musical idea, made some of the most intriguing scientific discoveries in the whole history of great ideas."

I didn't know then that Hindemith had this peculiar obsession with Kepler's life work — that for nearly a decade he had been fashioning an opera, *The Harmony of the World*, from the details of Kepler's dogged and bizarre life.

Again he went back to the ancient Greeks and their notion of the music of the spheres. Still rubbing his hands, he said: "The Pythagoreans imagined that each planet, in what they thought to be circular orbits, would sweep out a note, and that all their notes taken together produced a chord. There was, in their view, a constant cosmic chord sounding in the universe."

A faint glimmer of hope broke over me. Was there a truly celestial model of the music we humans hear down here on earth? And if so, how did he intend to connect this preoccupation with the history of science with the concerns of our class? "In a 1619 treatise," Hindemith went on, "Kepler published the first reliable scientific data showing that there are musical principles involved in the march of the planets around the sun. However, they are not as the ancient Greeks imagined them. Kepler's first law of planetary motion states that planets move in elliptical orbits at constantly changing rates of speed, and not in perfect circles at a constant velocity as the Greeks had thought. Further, the constantly changing relationships of the planets to each other cannot produce the single cosmic chord the Greeks had imagined."

Hindemith then read to us from a large book, *Harmonices Mundi*, the Kepler treatise of 1619 that he'd referred to earlier. Translating the Latin into English, he began: "The heavenly motions are nothing but a continuous song for several voices, to be perceived by the intellect, not by the ear; a music which, through discordant tensions, through syncopations and cadenzas, as it were, progresses toward certain predesigned six-voiced cadences, and thereby sets landmarks in the immeasurable flow of time."

What would Charlie Parker think of *this*, I wondered. Then Hindemith said that Kepler had thrown a challenge before the musicians of his own day — to set, to a sacred text, the musical march of the heavens, whose harmonies he could demonstrate in numbers — but the challenge was never met.

The clock on the wall said it was time to bring class to an end, and Hindemith summed up what he wanted to leave with us: "The science of music deals with the proportions objects assume in their quantitative and spatial, but also in their biological and spiritual, relations. Kepler's three basic laws of planetary motion could perhaps not have been discovered without a serious backing in music theory. It may well be that the last word concerning the interdependence of music and the exact sciences has not been spoken."

Feelings as strong as that, I've since learned, are sometimes as infectious as a virus. I surely was not aware of the extent of my own infection at first, but more than twenty-five years after I learned of Kepler's challenge to his musical contemporaries, and three and a half centuries after he first put it to them, the challenge still nagged at me as an itch demands a scratch. Hindemith's passion was now mine.

I was back at Yale's School of Music in 1979, this time as a professor, when it occurred to me that since Kepler's time — and Hindemith's — much had changed in music and in technology. With new developments like computers linked to tone generators and synthesizers it was possible, for the first time, to take up Kepler's challenge and make a precise realization "for the ear" of his astronomical data of 1619. I wanted passionately to hear the Keplerian "aural" planetarium. Since I didn't have the mathematical and astronomical skills to give expression in sound to Kepler's work, I enlisted a learned scientist friend, John Rodgers, a professor of geology at Yale and an accomplished musician. He mastered all the necessary elements for the completion of our task, and before long Mark Rosenberg, a graduate student at Princeton, used the data we provided to produce a computer program that gave us an audio tape.

Once Rodgers and I heard with our own earthly ears what Kepler and Hindemith had been so passionate about, yet had heard only with their intellects, we decided to release our realization of *The Harmony of the World* as a phonograph record. No large commercial record company carried such things; we would have to create our own. In tribute to the great and indomitable spirit of Johannes Kepler, whose nagging mother, throughout all of his troubled life, never tired of belittling his "idle scribblings" and predicting for him and his passion early and everlasting oblivion, we named our little record company The Kepler Label.

From the day the *New York Times* Tuesday Science Section carried the story of our work and the recording on its front page, our Yale switchboard buzzed with traffic; soon other scientific journals, and even the popular press, would refuse to let us rest. That, I think, would have made Paul Hindemith smile.

I was surprised to learn, shortly after becoming a student at Yale, that Paul Hindemith and I shared another passion. He'd had a lifelong love affair with the sound of the horn; and I, too, had long been partial to it. The quality of the horn's ancient and majestic clarion spoke directly to Hindemith's inner person.

I was thrilled to learn that an inspired horn performance could weaken his iron will and disrupt his otherwise disciplined and intensely ordered working routine. More than once a well-turned line played on the horn caused Hindemith to push all else aside and throw himself into feverish bouts of sketching.

One happy disruption fell on him while he toured Europe conducting orchestras in 1951. During the tour, four Salzburg hornists heard that the great Hindemith would soon pass through their village on a late-night sleeper. The night and the train carrying the sleeping Hindemith arrived. The four hornists waited trackside and gently blew a mellow four-part serenade, appropriate to the hour, just beneath the composer's window. Hindemith awoke at the sound and slid from his berth, bolting to the car's platform — still in his pajamas — for a closer hearing. The quartet thrilled him with well-harmonized chorales and German folksongs: they played on even as the train rolled away with the waving Hindemith beaming grateful cheers and encouragement while the horn players and their notes faded into the soft midnight.

For weeks the sound of the four-horn combination haunted him. He began putting pen to paper. His sketches filled his spare moments as he went about his duties. He found time to write fragments for four horns between work on important and long-overdue commissions.

Back in New Haven, a few months after the trackside horn serenade, Hindemith put the finishing touches on the new Sonata for Four Horns, which, during his next European tour, he would hand-deliver to the hornists who had inspired it.

A few days before leaving the country with the score, he assembled four student hornists in a Yale practice room. He wanted a read-through. My horn and I were privileged to play one of the parts.

His Horn Concerto had a similar birth. In 1949 Hindemith was in Europe enjoying a leave from Yale, and while there, he was invited to conduct a special orchestral concert. His anticipation was immense, for he was to have as his soloist the great English virtuoso of the horn, Dennis Brain. For weeks, it is said, he spoke of nothing else.

Hindemith would be hearing Dennis Brain in person for the first time, but the Mozart Horn Concerto they were to perform together was an old friend. Predictably, even as they rehearsed with the orchestra, Brain's artistry and elegant tone fanned Hindemith's old flame.

Just as predictably all else went to the back burner, even a handsome commission from Columbia University for an orchestral piece. Hindemith began sketching and orchestrating a new composition for horn and orchestra while working on the Columbia commission. Driven by his passion for Dennis Brain's sound, he finished the Concerto for Horn and Orchestra first.

There was something in the horn's call which evoked in Hindemith a longing for Old World values. These values he expressed in poems he composed for two of his most ambitious horn works, the Concerto for Horn and Orchestra and the Alto Horn Sonata. The sound of no other instrument had ever inspired such poetry from him. The poems he composed recall not only the values of a time long past but old and half-forgotten German words and usages long out of service, absent even from dictionaries since the Middle Ages.

> Mein Rufen wandelt
> In herbstgetönten Hain den Saal,
> Das Eben in Verschollnes,
> Dich in Gewand und Brauch der Ahnen,
> In ihr Verlangen und Empfahn dein Glück.

Gönn teuren Schemen Urständ,
Dir Halbvergessener Gemeinschaft,
Und mir mein tongestaltnes Sehnen.

My call transforms
The auditorium into an autumn-colored grove,
The now into the forgotten past,
You into the dress and customs of your ancestors,
Your happiness into their longing and resignation.
Grudge not the beloved ghosts their resurrection,
Nor yourself communion with them, the half-forgotten,
And me, my tone-inspired yearnings.

Hindemith's Alto Horn Sonata, for which he also composed a poem, had been written in 1943, six years earlier. It was composed during a short vacation with his wife in the small town of Egremont, Massachusetts, in the Berkshire Mountains. By then, the Berkshires had become a special comfort to Hindemith. He became attached to them while teaching at Tanglewood in the summers of 1941 and 1942, noting in some of his letters that parts of the Berkshires reminded him of the mountains of Switzerland.

I have often wondered why Hindemith chose to write this substantial and charming piece. The lowly alto horn has no solo repertoire. Though its voice is mellow and ever so musical, it has never been an instrument of status. Symphony orchestras have never had any use for it. No one has ever taken it seriously. It is the poor stepchild of the brass instrument family: band players of other instruments look on it with derision and call it the "peck horn." There is some justice in that, since the musical lines generally written for it are simpleminded syncopations played on afterbeats and on static, monotonous notes of the harmony — giving the impression of so much barnyard pecking. The alto horn is often confused with the mellophone, a kissing cousin of the French horn, and is more commonly found in the hands of schoolchildren and of lapsed trumpet players in military marching bands.

Hindemith was inspired by the memory of the call of the postman, who would announce his approach by blowing his horn as he made his rounds in the hamlets of Germany and Switzerland. "Das Posthorn" is the title of the poem of the Alto Horn Sonata. Even today, the posthorn is the official logo adorning mailboxes and railroad mail cars in Germany.

The Sonata for Horn and Piano of 1939, the first of Hindemith's solo works for the instrument, is a weightier work than the later two for which he wrote poetry. The seriousness of the times finds its way into the music of this work without the help of poetry. It was written in the small Swiss town of Bluch shortly after Hindemith learned that Germany had gone to war on 1 September 1939.

I decided last year to make a recording of all three of Hindemith's solo works for my instrument on one album. It had not been done before. I knew that I wanted to record the Concerto for Horn and Orchestra and the Alto Horn Sonata, both written during Hindemith's Yale years, making use of the great Newberry Memorial Organ in Woolsey Hall at Yale. I knew that Hindemith had come to know and appreciate that organ — its awesome versatility, its twelve thousand pipes, its vast range of textural possibilities. It is one of America's most important instruments.

I asked the arranger-orchestrator Sidney Fine, whose work I admire above all others', to make a four-hand piano reduction of the concerto's orchestra score. I was then introduced to Thomas Murray and listened to him play the mighty Newberry organ. He created the impression of a towering conductor in command of a great orchestra, and I began to imagine what the horn would sound like with this organ playing Fine's reduction of Hindemith's concerto. I thought of Dennis Brain and his great performance of the concerto with Hindemith as conductor. Then, for the first time in years, I remembered that Brain had also been an accomplished organist.

I went to Murray the next day and suggested that we use the organ and my horn in a recording of the concerto as a celebration of the art of both Hindemith and Brain. He began experimenting at the organ and registering Fine's reduction, scored for two players, and he was soon joined at the console by Durward Entrekin. (Murray also plays the Newberry organ in the Sonata for Alto Horn and Piano; for the recording of the Sonata for Horn and Piano I was joined by the distinguished Russian pianist Boris Berman.) It should surprise nobody that the recording was released on The Kepler Label.

Hindemith revealed yet another of his strongest musical passions in his History of the Theory of Music class. For him, a student's exploration of the great ideas in music theory from the past was incomplete, even irresponsible, without experiencing the music itself. That meant performing the musical output of the periods he covered. To my enormous impatience, he transcribed an endless stream of early European music dating from the twelfth to the sixteenth centuries and insisted that his students sing and play those transcriptions under his direction. He even insisted that we perform them on the original instruments, when available.

From somewhere out of the depths of Yale's darkest dungeons, Hindemith dredged up strange musical relics for us to play — shawms, sackbuts, krumhorns. These ancient wind instruments, dust-covered and hellishly out of tune, produced a music that brought no joy to their players and often sent the transcriber-conductor into cussing fits, during which he hurled at us a rich mixture of German and English invective. His message was clear in either language. Eventually, we began to make a sound that occasionally approximated music. Then we moved on up to the sixteenth century, and I longed for Charlie Parker to know what he was missing.

Hindemith set great store by the Venetian school, a sixteenth-century school of Flemish and (later) Italian composers at Saint Mark's. Inaugurated by Andrea Willaert of the Netherlands, the Venetian school included, among others, Andrea Gabrieli, Cypriano de Rore, Claudio Merulo, Giovanni Gabrieli, and Claudio Monteverdi. Hindemith thought highly of the work of two of the school's composers, whom he considered to be among the most progressive theorists of the time: Nicolo Vincentino and Gioseffo Zarlino.

When I first laid lip to the instrumental music of the Venetian school under Hindemith's direction, it was the work of Andrea Gabrieli, then that of his nephew Giovanni Gabrieli, that changed my mind about the presentness of the past in Venice. Giovanni's broad masses of sound, his polychoral treatment, his echo effects, and his extensive use of instruments together with voices, arrested my ear. Above all, I was intrigued by the majesty and complexity of his rhythms. I wondered then how such complex textures and rhythms could have been organized and performed five hundred years ago in that stone cathedral without the sound rolling aimlessly about and decaying into noisy confusion. Add that Gabrieli, as organist and composer for Saint Mark's, regularly wrote music for festive occasions in which he used several groups of performers strategically placed all around the building. Why did the sound of all this not run together like molasses and emerge a garbled blotch with echoes and dead spots, as we hear it in many of the newer halls around the world?

Since Saint Mark's musicians were so daring for their time, I suspected that its builders might have known something about acoustics which was not widely known in the rest of Europe, either then or now. Certainly the builders could not have had Gabrieli in mind when they laid out the plan for the church hundreds of years earlier. The music used for church services at that time was monophonic (a single sung melody), having no harmony and not even the accompaniment of an organ. By the early 1400s, six players of silver trumpets, who were paid by the Doge himself, had been hired in Saint Mark's. During the last two decades of the 1400s, the church received a second organ and gradually began to assume its place as a vital center in the development of European music.

A few summers ago I realized that thirty years had passed since I'd last become immersed in Hindemith's old musical passion. The Venetian school and Saint Mark's sprang to mind. A little voice urged: "Do something nice for your ears." Then I remembered that since Hindemith's class, something else of the Byzantine world, with Saint Mark's at its musical center, had found its way into my thinking.

Paul Robeson, who has long been my personal standard for artistry and musical scholarship, made a lifelong study of world music, and often sang songs from several parts of the world in his concerts — singing them always in their original languages to illustrate that the music of widely disparate lands springs from common roots. I knew a record from a concert he gave in Carnegie Hall in 1958 on which he sang an American Negro spiritual, a thirteenth-century plainchant from Czechoslovakia, an East African tribal chant, and an old Near Eastern Jewish chant whose melodies were nearly the same. Robeson's point was that there is a connection. And why? "Because," he said, "the Abyssinian Church and the Church of the Sudan were a part of the Eastern Church of Byzantium. Therefore, music from many parts of Africa and the Near East found its way into the liturgy of the early Byzantine church and from there, spread out into Europe."

Robeson made me realize the connection between spirituals, the first music I can remember hearing in my childhood household in Alabama, and other musics of the world. The notion of playing some of this interconnected music on my horn in an architecturally significant space began to excite me. And then it was clear. I could go to Venice and find a way to play my horn inside Saint Mark's. I'd play my spirituals and the plainchant from the *Liber Usualis*, "the book of use" containing the hymns and chants most used in the Catholic liturgy. Once again, one of Hindemith's musical passions re-emerged in me, became my own. What follows is a story about my horn and me, but I tell it now because it is also a story about Hindemith and certainly a part of my encounter with him.

Darkness was less than an hour away when I first arrived in Venice, and although Saint Mark's is only open to the public during the day, I decided to go and look at the outside of the church right away. I headed for Saint Mark's Square and walked all around it several times, keeping my eyes focused on the locked cathedral at its eastern end. I was already projecting my imagination into the next morning's work. Just to get myself warmed up, I paced off the approach to the main door of the cathedral from several directions, hoping that my sneakers would fall into the faded footsteps of Gabrieli, Monteverdi, Zarlino, and perhaps a sackbut-man or two. And I walked there for a very long time before jet lag said it was bedtime. That first night's sleep in the shadows of Saint Mark's was filled with dreams in which old Italian musicians blowing six silver trumpets spoke rapidly to me between phrases.

The following morning, still with the sound of the silver trumpets in my ear, I hurried back to the square, arriving just in time to find tourists from around the world lined up in front of the church.

I recalled all the polite Italian expressions I'd ever heard that might smooth the way of a man needing to get into the church in a big hurry. "Scusa, permesso, prego, scusa, prego," I pleaded — making an end run around the Swedes, nudging cautiously past the Germans, and slipping through the door. I must have given the impression of a man on a mission, for not a soul protested as I hit my stride, eyes fixed on the main altar. About midway down the aisle, still striding, I sensed an old but familiar discomfort come over me. I never know what to do with my hands when I face the altar in a Catholic church; and I am always confounded by the neat dipping at the knee that trained Catholics negotiate so expertly. Because I was brought up as a black Baptist in Alabama, I have a high reverence for all religious forms, symbols, and houses of worship; so to make peace I said a few more silent scusas, permessos, and pregos to the saints and hoped that my Baptist presence would not offend.

At last I was standing in the space where something important had first sounded five hundred years ago. I closed my eyes and tried to imagine the sound of the old singers and players. I breathed in great drafts of the

incense-laden air, shuffled the soles of my shoes across the geometric pat-
terns of the marble floors, and tried to sense in every pore — and especially
in the inner recesses of my ears — the essence and echo of Saint Mark's distant sound. I turned all the way around after several minutes and opened
my eyes. I was standing directly under the center dome of the five that compose the ceiling.

One of the oldest and best methods musicians use to test resonance
and echo duration is to clap their hands slowly and loudly. One cannot
be inconspicuous clapping loudly in Saint Mark's. I just closed my eyes
again, gave two resounding claps under the central dome, and listened:
WHAAACKKK. The first sound lasted undiminished in intensity for what
seemed a very long time, hanging in the air to linger through the second
clap. The slight difference between the two was clearly distinguishable; the
two beats merged together and slowly decayed. I repeated the test just to
make sure I was hearing what I thought I had heard. The sound came back
to me with all the sharpness of the blows mellowed out of it, sounding as
smooth as an organ note. I then moved all over the church repeating my
clap tests and ignored the looks of the other tourists when my whacks
drowned out their tour guides' talk.

After a while, I sat down to think about it all. I needed a plan. I had to
get permission to play at night when the place was closed up and quiet.
I'd not used the usual official channels for written permission to play in
church before leaving home and was trusting that the good luck that usually goes with me on musical quests would carry me through.

From the cool, comfortable stone bench where I sat, I saw a man dressed
in what looked like a doorman's uniform, standing reverently by the altar.
I approached him and asked when I might hear music in Saint Mark's.
"Only on Sundays, for the morning Mass," he said. I then asked if Sunday
was the only day during the whole week that music sounded in that
magnificent acoustical wonder. "Si," he said. I asked him what music, and
he told me that it was the sung Mass with choir and organ. I said that many
things had changed since Monteverdi and Gabrieli had been at Saint
Mark's. Raising both shoulders high, tilting his head while turning out both
palms, he said: "You speak of the time of the masters, Signore." Then it hit
me that, if Saint Mark's had fallen back to only one day a week for music,
I might have a tough time getting permission to do what I came for.

Back at my *pensione* I put the mute in my horn to soften its sound, and played through a few spirituals and a Sanctus and a Kyrie in the Lydian mode. Then I went back to Saint Mark's in the afternoon to make contact with the official who could give me permission to play there. The guard at the altar remembered me from earlier that morning, and said I must speak to Monsignore Semenzato. He was the business manager in charge of all such transactions as mine. I had brought with me a letter of introduction from Yale which solicited hospitality for me and attested that I was a scholar doing acoustical research in Venice. The letter was in English. I had also neatly folded a fifty-thousand-lire note in my shirt pocket to be presented as an offering which, legend has indicated, often opens church doors. But not right away. I waited. And waited.

Two days later, I still had my Yale letter and the fifty-thousand-lire note in my pocket. I was met at the door by Monsignore Semenzato, whose classic aristocratic good looks would not have been out of place in the Olivetti boardroom. Handing him my letter from Yale, I asked if he spoke English. He said he spoke a little French and handed the letter back. I said I would try to state my business in Italian. His look said, "You'd better make it good, Buster." I took a deep breath and started at the beginning. I was careful to take my time and sound out the long vowels in the names — Zarlino, Gabrieli, Merulo, Monteverdi — and try to make them sound as if they were my friends. His expression told me that my subject interested him about as much as a recitation of a recipe for bean salad. I paused to ask if my Italian was comprehensible. "Si, capito," he insisted. Then in a voice quite civil but with no charity, he asked, "What do you want to do?" I said I'd come to play and to make acoustical measurements in the church. The Reverend Father said, "The basilica is open. Go ahead. Play." I told him it couldn't be done with tourists there — I needed to come at night when the building was closed and silent.

His face changed and his speech quickened as he shifted to the local dialect. I caught practically nothing he said but his body language spoke volumes. Out of it all I kept hearing the word *arcidiacono*. Did it mean archdiocese? Must I go there? Was it in Venice, the Vatican? The interview was over.

Later that day, while having lunch in an outdoor café at Saint Mark's Square, I saw notices on the nearby walls that a concert of choral music by the Amherst College Glee Club would take place in Saint Mark's on the following night. Bill Zinsser had by then joined my venture, and I said to him,

"Somebody at Saint Mark's had to make arrangements for that concert. I'm going back in there and find him." We pushed our way through the crowd at the church's front door. This time I sought a janitor for information. Perhaps I'd started too high up in the front office with Monsignore Semenzato. I studied three or four sweepers and dusters, hoping to spot one with a face that smiled easily. Just such a man stood near the nave, leaning on his broom. I approached him, said where I was from, and told him my story. He said, "Surely — sounds interesting. Speak to my capo, he's right over there." I went to the boss-man my friend pointed out, and he, too, smiled easily. He stretched out his hand, and I shook it and began.

After I told him I was from an American university, all his answers to my questions were "Si, Professore" and "No, Professore." When I asked whom I should see to get permission to play in the basilica at night when it was quiet, he said, "Arcidiacono Spavento, Professore. No problem. You can speak to him here. He is always around here." He called out to one of his janitors: "Luigi, Spavento è scapato?" "Si, Capo, è scapato due minuti fa." Then to me he said, "Professore, as you heard my man say, Monsignore Spavento has left for the day, but he will be here tomorrow evening to hear confessions. Come to this side door at six o'clock tomorrow and I will introduce you. He's a nice guy." I was exhausted but happy. I needed the rest I'd earned that day, and Zinsser and I said good-bye for the night.

The next night at six o'clock I entered by the side door and found the capo. He was expecting me and led me directly to a confessional in a side chapel. He pulled back the curtain and whispered something. I heard a slight movement inside, behind the curtain — a soft shuffle of feet, the rustling of cloth. The capo whispered that an American professor was there to speak to Monsignore, and when he pulled the curtain all the way back, I saw a very old priest slumped down in his chair. He had been asleep. He had very white hair; his face looked old and tired.

When I saw that his tongue was working in the side of his mouth in the rhythmical way of a person who's had a stroke, I thought, "That does it. I'm dead." But I started my speech from the beginning, speaking of Willaert the Netherlander and then his Italian successors. I could see that the names of Gabrieli, Monteverdi, Zarlino, and the others were having an effect: the more such names I reeled off, the more the priest sat up in his chair. I talked on, and he became tall and straight. It looked as though years fell from his tired old face. His tongue stopped working and his eyes brightened. When I mentioned the near-perfection of Saint Mark's acoustics, he held up his index finger and wagged it before his face, interrupting me: "Scusa, Profes-sore, Saint Mark's acoustics are perfetto! Per-fet-to!"

I could see an almost puzzled bemusement in the Monsignore's face. I imagined he had been waiting for years for someone to come to talk to him of his beloved church. He looked up at me and asked softly, "What do you want to do here?" I told him I needed time in the church at night—alone, in silence—and that I wanted to bring a recording machine and play the horn there as the musicians in Gabrieli's time had done. That was the only way I knew to explore the sound qualities that have mystified musicians through the centuries. "How much time?" I told him that two hours would be enough. He paused a moment, rubbing the stubble on his chin, and then called to the capo, who had been listening nearby. They discussed my problem in the rapid Venetian dialect, and then the arcidiacono asked, "Is tomorrow night soon enough for you?" I said it was per-fet-to. He told me to come to the side door at seven-thirty after Mass the next night, when the church would be mine, and I was prepared to thank him and leave. But he took my hands in his and asked, "Tell me, are you a Latin American?" I had felt his eyes examining my face and head. Guessing that he'd not seen many who looked as I do, I said, "No, sir, I am from North America, a mix of African and American." He squeezed my hand harder and asked, "You are an Afro-American?" "Yessir, I am." "Well, this is the first time I have met an Afro-American. It has long been one of my convictions that the Mediter-ranean world with its rich cultural mixes has shaped much of what is intrig-uing in Western civilization. From there came the cultural influences that are at work in the best of Europe. That is why Saint Mark's is so unique. This basilica itself is such a mixture." He chuckled wistfully for a moment and then went on. "What an idea! Wouldn't it be fantastic if the glorious musical story of this church were to be brought back to the attention of the world through the interest and deep appreciation of an Afro-American!"

Finally he let go of my hand. I felt the loss. But I left the church smiling because I thought of the English translation of the old priest's name: *spavento* means "fright"!

At seven-thirty next evening, Zinsser and I were at the side door. The capo had left for the day. His assistant led us into the empty church. Being alone there at that hour with the fading twilight streaming through the colored windows gave the church an atmosphere that was almost eerie in its majesty and beauty.

I went to work immediately according to a plan I'd begun laying the first day I came to the church. I turned on the recorder, took my horn, and stood under the center dome. Even with the church empty, it was not silent. There were minute creaks and shivers — the sound of groaning stone — evidence that the marble edifice was cooling off and settling down for the night. I took a long moment, even with the tape rolling, to listen to the near-silence.

I blew my first note, a C, neither long nor short. I was just barely breathing the wind into the instrument, yet the note went on flying and ringing long after I'd quit pushing. It felt clear and easy. There was the expected echo — but I also heard a tone quality far richer and warmer than any I'd heard from my horn before. My note had gone searching out all the surfaces of Saint Mark's and then came back to my ears culled of dross, with only the purest overtones remaining. The echo seemed to come from everywhere.

Staying with the same note, I moved from dome to dome and all around the nave and alcoves. By the time I'd finished my test, I had gained some understanding of the sound characteristics of Saint Mark's and why they were special. It was clear that music-making there had to be a transaction of restraint and soft-pedalling. Above all, tempos, volume, and dynamics must be allowed to set themselves. The basilica itself is an instrument. It was clear that Saint Mark's has to be *played* — not just played in.

Now I was ready to play. My first station would be the main choir loft, high up over the front entrance. I had already marked my selections in the *Liber Usualis* and had chosen four spirituals to play. These I knew by heart.

I played first an Agnus Dei I'd heard at the Vatican. From up high, the horn sound was even more enveloping. Since the microphone was so far away from me, I thought to project the horn's tone slightly. When I later listened to what I'd played I discovered that I need not have made allowances for the distance. I should have remembered to trust Saint Mark's to play itself.

Darkness was falling as I left the high choir loft. The sacristan brought candles to light my station in the nave at a small altar at the side of the church. When the church's tower clock struck nine, I had finished playing from the book. I still had half an hour to try out my spirituals.

I began with "Were You There When They Crucified My Lord?" I cannot describe the ways this song differs from the Masses I'd read from the book. I can only say that I was aware of standing on holy ground, a mere thirty feet from the remains of Mark, and that my thoughts were in my family's

Baptist church in Alabama. My horn was the rich contralto voice of Miss Celie Appleton, our town's best singer, and the sound I had made was as close as I've ever come to Miss Celie's.

When I'd played the last note of the song, the sacristan reappeared with a friend in tow. He said, "Bene! Com'è bella!" He and his friend wanted to know what the music was. That the song was Afro-American and that its origins shared something with Saint Mark's surprised and delighted them. He asked me to play more and the two of them sat on a marble bench to listen. As I played the next song, both of my auditors jerked their heads in the changing directions of the sound, as if trying to follow the flying echo with their eyes.

After I'd played "Go Down, Moses" and "Give Me Jesus," my energies were spent. I had ten more minutes on the clock, so I played through a few melodies of a Bach cello suite and then packed away my horn and recording gear.

The sacristan offered to let me go on playing. I thanked him, but declined. It would have been meaningless. I had already done my best. And I was satisfied, finally, that my old horn — the same one I'd used when Hindemith first made us play Gabrieli — and I had turned the nighttime silence of Saint Mark's into music. It was Paul Hindemith's moment as well as mine.

STANLEY CAVELL

Notes after Austin

When in the early 1950s I came from California to Harvard for graduate study in philosophy, the grip of logical positivism was loosening a little with age and success. The new thing in question — this was before the translation into English of Wittgenstein's *Investigations*, and while Heidegger and Continental philosophy in general were still largely rumor to American philosophers — was the so-called philosophy of ordinary language, represented by a seemingly endless supply of papers from a seemingly endless supply of talented philosophers at Oxford. Many young teachers of philosophy here, and, it seemed, most of the really promising graduate students I was meeting, were finding ways to spend at least a year working at Oxford. I had not wanted to. I was too unsettled in my relation to the profession of philosophy to know whether time at Oxford or rather in France and Germany was more to the point for me.

Then after J. L. Austin came to Harvard as the William James Lecturer in the spring of 1955, I felt I already had a life's work ahead of me — at least so far as the claim of the ordinary, that mode of thinking of which he was the purest representative, would enter it. The purity was clear enough from his essay "Other Minds," a miniature encyclopedia of ordinary language concerns; and it was testified to by tales from those returning each year from Oxford about the weekly discussions Austin held for the young teachers of philosophy there, one of which he reportedly gave over entirely to the distinction between signing "Yours sincerely" and "Yours truly." But it took his presence for me to come to experience his inexhaustible interest in what he called the jump of words — an interest arising (I of course supposed) from an inexhaustible faith in the philosophical yield of the details of the language we share and that shares us, and yet a faith that also turned in a direction somewhat opposite, to face the concerns of linguists and of poets. Like linguistics and poetry, Austin's philosophizing, I felt, allowed me — demanded of me — the use of myself as the source of its evidence and as an instance of its conclusions. Whatever philosophy's pertinence to me, I felt for the first time my pertinence to philosophy; I stopped looking for ways to leave the subject.

The year after Austin's semester at Harvard I returned to California to begin teaching, so it happened that I was present with Austin also during the other semester he spent in America, at Berkeley in 1959, the year before he died, not yet fifty. My memories of him are accordingly solely and fully American.

I have had other teachers, as well as friends and students, with wider learning, or greater creative sweep, or smarter powers of reasoning, but I have encountered no one with a clearer and more constant fastidiousness of mind, joined with a respect for the vicissitudes of daily life — call it moral imagination. The thinkers I admire most have this joint power. Sometimes, I know, I prefer thinking that allows more of the darkness of its findings to appear than Austin's does. But I suppose darkness is nothing, or useless, without something of the lightness, the freedom of mind, that Austin demanded of himself and expected of his students. I had after college "given up" (so I called it) music for philosophy. Working in Austin's classes was the time for me in philosophy when the common rigors of exercise acquired the seriousness and playfulness — the continuous mutuality — that I had counted on in musical performance. This may have meant to me that what was happening in Austin's classes was not, as it lay, quite philosophy; but I was at the moment too happy with whatever it was to have cared. That Austin's practice had to do, in its own way, with the possession of an ear, was surely part of its authority for me. (Here I have to think through the fact that my mother was a professional pianist, with perfect pitch, while my father was musically illiterate.)

Others found Austin cold. Of the legends that formed around him a number had to do with a quality that might strike you as coldness, but perhaps rather as reserve or even strictness. Some concerned a certain awe he inspired by his work in army intelligence during the Second World War. Then there was the story about Austin as eccentrically pure teacher, told by a colleague with whom he gave one of his classes. Attendance had fallen with each week's session until at the final meeting, before Christmas break, it fell to zero. The colleague made as if to leave, but Austin insisted — stated rather, or perhaps simply reminded them both — that they had contracted themselves to do philosophy for this period, and that he intended to do it. So the two of them talked philosophy together for the assigned time. I experienced Austin's relentlessness over the course of falling attendance at his William James Lectures, the primary obligation of his invitation to Harvard. The lectures were entitled "How to Do Things with Words." How, I felt, could it have dawned on so few a number — not more at the end than one in twenty of the several hundred who had begun the course, or anyway who came to the initial lecture — that something of world-historical significance was happening here? But there are worse forms and causes of reception. And some people knew. Enough.

I also experienced a version of the strictness. Already full of admiration for Austin, and already feeling some credit with him for my knack at producing examples he found pertinent, I responded impatiently, during a discussion at lunch in Adams House with a circle of students, to a question concerning whether something must be common to things sharing a common name, saying, in effect, "If people want to say there are universals, let them. It doesn't matter as long as they know the facts." I was sitting next to Austin, and he turned toward me as if startled, and said hard, straight between the eyes, "It matters." I felt an utter, quite impersonal, shame — shame, and a kind of terror, as if before the sacred task of philosophy, for having been faithless to its calling. Whatever the values to be assessed in this exchange, whatever the chances of illusion or romance, personal coldness is hardly the issue. How could mere coldness have lasted, have profited me, to this moment?

Rarely in a lifetime can one know intellectual gratitude of the kind I felt toward Austin after his first seminar meeting on the subject of excuses. I left elated, as if I had been shown a route out of the realm of arbitrary, massive demands for consent, as if I were tasting intellectual liberty, my own intelligence, for the first time. No doubt it was not the first; and it will not be the last. But it remains astounding that it happened with respect to such seemingly trivial matters. Those matters remain as hard to convey as ever, but (to my mind) it is no less necessary to continue to try to do so.

The matter of ordinary language philosophy — its content, so to speak — is trivial, is nothing, without its method(s). In practice the gratitude for the seminar was for the continuous pleasure of discovery and agreement, for the community of purpose Austin's work suggested as he laid out a geography of concepts ranging from the tyrants of philosophical thought—intention, will, consequence, reality—to the all but unnoticeable workers and operatives of everyday thinking life, such as heedlessness, thoughtlessness, inadvertence, and the mistaken and the accidental. He was going over matters he had gone into more thoroughly than anyone else; he was a master of something. This was no longer the provision of a great result or paradigm of philosophical thought such as Russell's Theory of Descriptions, building on Frege's invention of the quantifier, which we were then to apply with endless unoriginality to a thousand identical situations. The questions raised here are to be decided by us, here and now. No one knows more about what mistakes and accidents are, or heedlessness or lack of thought, than we do, whatever we think we do or do not know. It is a frightening, exhilarating prospect.

Sometimes I disliked Austin's handling of contention. Not even he could always get beyond the note of the personal, of fear produced from outside, as from mere force, and not from my sense that I am bound to know, that somehow one already knew. But to my mind there were moments in Austin's seminar of perfect spiritual tact, as on the day, after his stories to distinguish among excuses such as doing something mistakenly, accidentally, heedlessly, and so forth, when he distinguished among modifiers such as something's being just or simply or purely an accident (one, say, in which nothing further, or nothing more complex, is in play, or mixed in) and a mere or sheer accident (one to which you could be assigning undue significance, or one whose accidental quality is transparent). A student interjected that *sheer* could not mean *transparent* because there is such a thing as sheer wool. Austin was taken by surprise, lifted his pipe from his mouth, and asked intently, "Is there? What is it?" The answer began immediately, but continued with a distinct ritardando: "Well, it's a weave you can see through." It was the sort of shocking moment, here in the hilarity of its sheer contradiction, that might cause conversion. Indeed it is my view that the power of the philosophical appeal to ordinary language is always only to be appreciated by an overcoming of resistance, which is to say by conversion—an appreciation, I mean, at once of the apparent triviality of the appeal and of the radical revelation of its successes. Without now seeking to comprehend the state of the student who as it were did not know that *sheer* continued to go with *transparent* even when applied to wool (as if the very meaning of wool contains the idea of opacity and as if mere ordinary words, such as *mere* or *sheer*, could not possibly be so controlled as for example to transfer their figure and everyday energy intact, without our realizing it, from silk or cotton to wool); and without now seeking to formulate the state of the student's understanding that the transfer had after all happened (as if the prior state of conviction that it could not happen is part of our agreement that what happens to us is inherently trivial, that we live as if our daily experience were not ours, or just because ours, of no general significance): I recall here the moment of Austin's response to the explanation, "Well, you can see through it," a moment I described as of spiritual perfection. The eyes that had been fixed wide with attention were now almost closed, and wrinkled at the corners, with satisfaction; the lips were pursed as if to keep from letting forth laughter; and the pipe came back up, the tip not quite to the mouth but to be punched lightly and repeatedly against the chin. Here was serious mirth in progress, and what I read as perfection was the projection of my utter faith, then and now, that the mirth was impersonal, that here a class had witnessed not the private defeat of an individual's experience but the public victory of sweet and shared words — mirth over the happy fact that the world is working out and that we are made for it. I suppose I again romanticize a moment. Then a form my gratitude to Austin takes is for the power of such moments, and successors of them, to bear this romance.

My daughter Rachel was two years old the fall Austin was in Berkeley. He once came to our house carrying a box of colored pencils and a drawing tablet, neither of them wrapped, and after saying hello went at once to the coffee table, knelt on the floor before it, and began to draw. Rachel joined him and received some pencils and paper in case she too wanted to draw. By the time they finished comparing sketches it was somehow clear whose pencils and papers these had become.

Seeing this and knowing that Austin had four children (his devotion to his family and to his farm were also the subjects of legend) I was moved to mention something to him that I felt pressed by and which I was not able to talk to others productively about. I said in effect that I found myself full of philosophical confusion and ambition that I would gladly give all my time to, and found myself at the same time glad to be committed for a lifetime to caring for a child. A banal anxiety, no doubt itself as confused as my feelings about philosophy. What Austin said was: "They keep one young." Was that a wise or a banal (call it merely an ordinary) thing to say? I found it better than either, because responsive. It responded to my evident wish to know how he handled the issue, or rather whether it was an issue for him. I took his response to signify that it was of course an issue, that I was not silly to feel pressed by it, but that since, like him, I was a father, I had better accept that fact into my normal day — into (if it comes to that) my philosophical confusion and ambition. And I took him further to be offering some such piece of advice as this: Do not expect or need to say or to hear something interesting about what is not out of the ordinary; the struggle you speak of is common, and the struggle is worthwhile. But that is exactly, so I felt and feel, what I wanted to hear from him.

Someone may take it that I draw too much Zen out of this plainness. Then still once more that is a form my gratitude bears toward Austin, a form it is for me to know he would bear.

Something of the gratitude can arise fresh at any time I feel the pretension and emptiness of the din of claims to advanced theories (say, in the field of literature, among others) that seem to me at once to know nothing of the difficulties of plainness and to function as defenses against them. And then there is another level of gratitude for Austin's plainness — his philosophical willingness to be ignorant. If sometimes this meant he did not wish to muse upon the darker side of the world, it also showed his healthy terror of it — he whose expertise in army intelligence concerned German matters — along with his contempt for those who toy with it, as perhaps he felt Wittgenstein too much did, or encouraged.

I write this on the flight back from a week's glimpse of Japan. During the obligatory twenty-four hours in Kyoto I learn, after a fragmentary Bunraku puppet performance, that a conference on Zen Buddhism is in progress there. It is for me to know the un-Zen-like spirit in which the thought crossed my mind that Austin's work would probably not have been cited at this conference. (I have some sense of why business gets big, and why big physics is called for; but what good are big theology and big philosophy?)

The Bunraku puppet that was presented for us — a female figure named Oshichi in a gorgeous robe — was carried centrally by one man, with her robes and props managed by two additional men whose bodies were completely clothed and whose heads completely wrapped in black cloth (were

they men?). The moment of crisis is brought on by Oshichi's reading a
letter. Who reads the letter? Reading here is an intentional act. Whose intention is it? I believe Austin would have accepted an answer that I believe
Wittgenstein would have accepted: "*She* reads it, of course," meaning
Oshichi. But Austin's reserve must be imagined in play. He is on record as
urging such thoughts as this: You can say a cloud looks exactly like a camel
(he may even have allowed that a cloud can *be* a camel) exactly because
you know that a cloud is not (and looks nothing like) a camel. Here you
glimpse something of what the concept of looking like depends on: an
unquestioned sense of the practical systems of contrasts between realities
and appearances, not on one general contrast between appearances and
nonappearances. And I imagine he might have been willing to urge this:
You can say Oshichi reads the letter exactly because you know that the
puppet—the thing in gorgeous cloth worked by three men—is not a thing
that reads. Here you glimpse something of what the concept of intention
depends on: an unquestioned sense of who owns the intentions of one's
actions, which seems to suppose that one owns one's actions, or at least
some of them. Suppose I say that in the case of the puppet you do not
know—are meant not to know—whether the puppet obeys the men or,
since every movement of the men serves the demands of the puppet,
whether the men obey the puppet. If life were this way ordinarily, our concept of intention would in a sense be empty, hollowed out. That Austin
would perhaps not affirm this possibility is to my mind less important than
that his writing, in the very goodness of its humor, is at every moment obedient to it.

I would like to assume that anyone interested in such matters will see,
or come to see, in the response I have imagined, its bearing on the communications Derrida and Searle traded some years ago concerning Austin's
disturbed footnote that remembers—as if suddenly—some hollowness in
performative utterances on, among other places, the stage. From that date
Austin seems to have come under the protection rather of the literary than
of the philosophical profession. Whatever the justice here, the cost of this
protection—so far—has been, from my angle, exorbitant, because the
literary profession takes it—so far—that ordinary language is contrasted
in Austin with *literary* language, whereas its contrast and contest is with
words as they appear in *philosophy* (if you can spot that). Austin for the
literary profession is to that extent not real but toy or stuffed or a decoy.

The time of Austin's departure from Harvard came within a few days of the Society of Fellows annual picnic and softball game. I thought Austin might enjoy ending on this note among others, and he accepted my invitation with interest. When we arrived the softball game was already in progress and it was somehow understood that if we wished to play, we should join the team batting and take our at bats at once. Austin could have seen enough from the play as we approached the field to recognize roughly what the batter was meant to do, if not fully why; if he had not seen enough he would decline. In response to my hesitating glance and gesture toward home plate, Austin walked to it, took off his suit jacket and laid it neatly aside on the grass, leaving his tie in place and his French cuffs closed. His stance seemed stiff, the knees were too straight and the bend from the waist crowded the plate. I felt certain he was going to swing at the first pitch if he could possibly react to it—there was no umpire and he was informed that he could look at pitches without cost to himself. He hit the pitch sharply over the second baseman's head and as he rounded first he touched the base smartly with his hand. I thought he should have stopped there but he made it to second standing up. I was of all things most surprised by how fast he was, and as I write this I still seem to see him standing on second with a trace of a smile, as if with an appropriate pride at a moment exactly realized, the world working out and we made for it.

That was thirty-two years ago, outside Boston. Half a century before that, in Poland, outside Bialystok, there had evidently been no call for my father, about fourteen the year his family sailed for America, to learn to hit to the opposite field. But I have known for a while now that my affinity for ordinary language philosophy and Austin's practice of it was prepared by my father's reaching, say, the point of my birth with no language ordinary or natural to him (the old gone or frozen, the new broken from the beginning); and by his nevertheless being famous in our small circle as I was growing up for his ability to tell stories full of leavening pleasure in a life on the move, and of argumentative pertinence. So he was part of the conditions of felicity in my invitation to Austin to that picnic, part of why I was in the position to extend it. Then, reciprocally, Austin's happy double entered into and has eased the long journey of forgiving my father his suffering.

MONROE ENGEL

An Exemplary
Edmund Wilson

I suppose now, in retrospect, that my twenty-year acquaintance with
Edmund Wilson was filial in character — elective filial, with the happy
advantages of such free relationships. We met first in Princeton in 1952
when I was a late-starting graduate student and he was giving a set of Christian Gauss seminars coming out of his research for *Patriotic Gore*. I had
just published my first novel and considered myself a citizen of the world
of letters masquerading as a graduate student, but that was not, I now
know, quite how I looked to Edmund. In a letter to Allen Tate dated
November 23, 1952, he writes: "We went to dinner the other night with
some young people who are living in your old house in Linden Lane. The
place was rather bare, and it made me sad at first — I missed Caroline's
romping dachshund and your old Confederate flag that used to hang in the
back room. They are using for a nursery the room that you used as a dining
room and in which I remember some wonderful dinners. It all seems longer
ago than it ought to."

My wife and I were those "young people" and we then had three children,
the oldest of whom was not yet five. The house on Linden Lane had been
a great find for us, at once small but roomy, and to our minds it was not
really bare but uncluttered. The four rooms on the first floor opened one
to another in a circle around an odd central staircase that branched front
and back, and on inclement days, or when they were just charged up, our
children and dog could course that circle in file at an accelerating pace until
they'd worked off enough steam to be ready for more peaceful occupation.
The former dining room that Edmund referred to as a nursery we called
a playroom, and it had a much-used, often-mended fishnet that hung under
the ceiling and from which various colorful or otherwise attractive objects

were suspended. We ate in the back room that had previously been dedicated to the Tates' Confederate flag.

It was incontestable, though, that we had very little furniture, and that what we had was austere and inexpensive, though our Eames and Aalto chairs have now, I recently discovered, become collectors' items. On the evening in question, Edmund had settled on a sling chair — canvas on a rod frame — as, probably, the most comfortable chair in the living room, but when his short-legged, full-bellied torso dropped into the sling, he was tipped back so that his natural field of vision was on the ceiling. At one moment, though, while he was talking from this posture, he flung himself forward to cover a sneeze, and discovered that our oldest child, Robin, had brought her own miniature sling chair into the living room and positioned herself right next to him. He at once broke off what had been more or less a lecture he'd been giving, apologized to her for having overlooked her — which was literally what he had done — and volunteered to perform a piece of magic for her that he'd done previously with great success, he said, in many parts of the world. He then knotted his handkerchief into a semblance of a mouse that he nested in his hand with its head, propelled by a finger, alternately poking nervously out of and retracting back into this nest. He did this, to my surprise, so skillfully, that Robin still believed weeks later that he had by magic produced a live white mouse.

Perhaps I remember this incident out of an evening that has otherwise lost detail as vividly as I do not only for its oddness, but also because it was my first view of certain unexpected and winning aspects of Edmund's character that I was to see a lot of later — his love of simple fun, his rather formal courtesy that alternated with that more frequently noted directness that could easily feel like rudeness, his according of attention to people without reference to their age or importance.

We didn't meet again after this year in Princeton until 1960, when Edmund and his wife Elena rented one of the end houses in a row of houses on Hilliard Street in Cambridge all but directly across from the house my wife and I had bought in 1955 when we moved from Princeton to Cambridge. We had a fourth child by then, but nonetheless our family was significantly older than it had been eight years earlier, and our house here was both more fully and less provisionally furnished. Hilliard Street was a neighborly street, and the Wilsons quickly became neighbors. They had a daughter, Helen, who was Robin's age, and the rather large gang of children on the street who played together regularly brought their parents into some informal exchange. Edmund and I soon learned each other's working habits, and knew when to drop in for the gossip we both appreciated after a day of solitary work. I liked to get him to talk about books or about writers he'd known, which he liked to do, and did in a wonderfully immediate way that depended on his capacity for vivid recall. He'd report a conversation with "Scott" or "Dos" as though it had taken place sometime earlier in the week, and I'd experience a distinct frisson of immediacy when he said, for example, "Zelda could never stand Ernest anyway." But I also enjoyed the privilege of personal instruction, as on the occasion when we'd all gone one evening to see the Piccolo Teatro di Milano do a marvelous production of Goldoni's *A Servant of Two Masters* at Sanders Theatre. After the performance, we came back to our house for a drink, and Edmund entertained and edified us for half an hour or more with a history of the tradition of pantomime on which Goldoni was building.

A regular part of what we did when we saw each other was exchange news of anything that might be freshening to see or hear — a movie, a play, a concert — only this could sometimes lead to trouble between us. I once recommended a Cassavetes film to him that I'd liked, and the next evening he appeared at my door later than he would usually have come without calling first and in a state of considerable pique. He had just returned from seeing the movie, and had to report that he'd found it a barely tolerable bore. Stung, I fired back, and after a moment he began to laugh and told me that he'd been reminded of similar controversies he'd had with his mother when he was young, only now he was on the other side. Several times too, in the interest of amusement and vivification, he gave memorable combined magic and Punch and Judy shows for us and a few other of his younger friends and their children. He was an accomplished magician and puppeteer, avocations that he applied himself to with seriousness and energy and to which he brought a degree of manual dexterity, evident to me first in his mouse trick, for which nothing else about the way his body did and didn't serve him would have prepared me.

It took me a while, though, to realize that Edmund's hunger for amusement was whetted by a harsh consciousness. In 1960 he was sixty-five, the same age, I'm startled to realize, that I am now. That he lived another twelve years is a miracle — or, put more realistically, evidence of extraordinary determination to go on, though without much simultaneous wish to take care of himself in any restrictive fashion. He was in prematurely bad shape — overweight, gouty, and with a number of less obvious but more threatening ailments, not least among them a bad heart — and he also had an absolute apprehension of being a survivor in a world that no longer made sense or felt immediate to him. This had been given full expression five years earlier in *A Piece of My Mind: Reflections at Sixty*; and a couple of years earlier still, in his obituary essay on Edna St. Vincent Millay, with whom he'd been tormentingly in love when he was a young man, he writes of dreaming of her one night in 1950, the night after she'd died but before he'd known of her death, a dream he thought might have been telepathic but was at least "partly motivated, no doubt, by my wanting, in my sleep, to have somebody to listen to my literary gossip and somebody from old times to talk to."

Watching him now, increasingly I found myself having to anticipate what it would be like to be betrayed in time by my own body. He slipped once on the ice when we were walking together, in one of those Cambridge winters of which his detestation is a matter of record, and when I caught him the only way I could, by one arm, and apologized for the pain I knew this must have caused him, he snorted and said, "Nonsense, my dear boy, you saved me!"

He addressed me as "my boy" or "my dear boy" when, I think, the historical distance between us was most palpable, when he could feel the comparative deficiencies in my knowledge of life. Once he expressed bewilderment about the problems he was having editing his notebooks — he was uncertain both about what he wished to publish, and about what he could — and I said that if he'd let me read one or two of the notebooks I'd be better able to consider these issues. "My dear boy," he said, dismissing this possibility out of hand, "if I let you read any of this, you'd never let me in your house again." Not literally true, of course, which he knew as well as I did, but his hunch that I might well not respond usefully to what I read has been more or less confirmed by my reading of the notebooks as they've been published.

His body was failing and his zest for life was flickering. He returned to Paris for a visit and was desolated. The city had changed abominably, he reported. He'd witnessed a demonstration in which the carbon monoxide in the air under the Arc de Triomphe had killed a caged rat in less than an hour. But the real change, he then told me once, was in himself. He was old.

To me he seemed not so much old as worn, and I saw that his continuing appetite for intellectual life was insatiable even when all else failed. And for intellectual combat. In the 1960s, after all, he continued to publish significant literary essays on, among other subjects, Russian literature and Canadian literature, and he also engaged in rousing polemics against the Internal Revenue Service and the Modern Language Association. An incident that occurred in the spring of 1962, though, caused me to focus both on just how under threat he felt, and on the rage with which he could sometimes respond to that threat. The time was mid-April, one of those first spring nights warm enough to cause us to open our bedroom windows instead of just cracking one of them more or less piously, as we do in winter. That means, though, since we have almost no front yard and our windows are right over the narrow street, that street sounds are vividly audible once more and have to be readapted to. The richness of the sensory atmosphere on these first mild nights exercises a summons to which it's almost impossible to respond adequately, and that difficulty, I find, does not decrease with age. What brought us rather terrifyingly awake this time, however, at around two in the morning—not much like anything I'd ever heard coming from that street before—was a series of wordless bellows that the common forms of anger couldn't account for. This wasn't simply anger, it was rage. The word can seem literary only until such time as you actually hear that emotion give voice. But we had little time to think about what we were hearing before the telephone next to our bed rang. When I picked it up, Elena Wilson identified herself and asked in a tone in which I could hear both concern and disapproval—a combination I was to hear frequently in the next several years when she thought Edmund was treating himself badly—whether I knew a doctor who would respond to a call for help at this hour of the night.

Fortunately, and against all odds, I did. Our family physician, Louis Zetzel, was that rare, kind bird who would still make house calls when there was reason to. I telephoned him and explained what little I knew of the situation, and we arranged to meet on the street in front of the Wilsons' house. Shortly after I'd pulled on my previous day's clothing again and gotten out there, Lou appeared in his car. Unlike me, he was cleanly shaved and punctiliously dressed. He wasn't wearing a tie, but this omission suggested urgency rather than informality.

Elena, who had been watching for us, let us into the house without our having to ring the bell or knock. Disturbed but somehow also amused or ironic, shifting her weight stiffly and excitedly from leg to leg as she talked — she'd broken either one or both knees in athletic accidents when she was young — and with her arms and hands held straight down at her sides, she told us that Edmund had been in pain for some hours; that in the course of the evening he'd had quite a lot to drink, which hadn't helped; that he was angry enough to have thrown various objects, including his typewriter, against the walls of his bedroom. There was a continuous overtone of amused disapproval in this account. Worldly and knowing, Elena was never surprised by anyone's behavior, but she gave good and bad grades for behavior nonetheless. I assumed she had expressed her disapproval to Edmund in less amused fashion when I heard her say she couldn't guarantee that he'd allow himself to be examined but thought the chances of a successful meeting between doctor and patient better if Lou went upstairs now alone.

Though less frequent and less violent than the bellows that had awakened me a little earlier, the sounds issuing from the second floor of the house were still not promising, and Lou climbed the stairs with obvious and understandable hesitancy while Elena and I remained alert below. We were prepared to mount too if we were needed but hoped that we wouldn't be — and, in my case at any event, very uncertain about what would happen if we were. Lou must have reached the bedroom door and halted when we heard his footsteps and the emanations of Edmund's anger cease more or less at the same instant. "Who are you?" Edmund boomed after a moment with distinct hostility.

"A physician!" Lou answered, a characteristic break or quaver in his voice that was a mature version of an adolescent sound. "Are you in pain?"

Another silence ensued before we heard Edmund address Lou as his dear boy, and tell him that for the past several hours he'd entertained pains that, with due respect, he thought no physician was likely even to know names for. I relaxed then (and I thought Elena did, too), reasonably confident that the necessary introduction had been effected and that Lou would be allowed to do whatever he considered immediately necessary. The voices floating down the stairwell were both now quieter, businesslike, so that we couldn't hear what was being said.

When Lou rejoined us after five or ten minutes, he reported that there was no immediate medical crisis, and that he'd given Edmund a shot that should ease his pain sufficiently to allow him to go to sleep. That wouldn't, he thought, take long, but he wasn't going to leave until it had happened.

So the three of us now sat together in the living room, waiting. I can no longer remember what we talked about or even how long we sat there. Fifteen minutes, half an hour. Probably Elena offered to make us coffee or tea and we declined to have anything. Probably she didn't offer us a drink, which we would also have declined. There was no resumption of alarming sounds overhead. At first nothing at all was audible. Then, though, we began to hear stirrings — identifiable sounds of bedclothes sliding across each other and the creaking of bedsprings. As these became more frequent, Lou explained to us that the medication he'd administered could sometimes have a paradoxical effect. Instead of encouraging sleep, it could make the patient wakeful. I've since wondered, thinking about this, whether that effect wasn't triggered by the patient's will — whether the reduction of pain didn't stimulate Edmund to want not sleep but renewed activity. But whatever the cause, we soon heard feet planted on the floor, followed by the slow but determined shuffle of slippers out of the bedroom and along the hall to the stairs.

The ensuing descent was very slow. For some years walking had been a problematic activity for Edmund at best, and he was not now at his best. But the other side of that audible absence of physical confidence was an equally audible determination, what is aptly called dogged determination and is the only quality I've come to believe that can make old age anything but a progressive concession to less and less. We saw first Edmund's slow, slippered feet on the stairs as he descended, then his pajama legs, then the bathrobe that didn't quite close over his portly center, and then finally the massive, avian, predatory head on the short neck, with lines of determination visible along the jowly jaw. The head was inclined to check footing, but I imagine that Edmund couldn't see his feet, screened as they were from him by his stomach, more than intermittently. Toward the bottom of the stairs there was a landing and a ninety-degree turn, and when he'd accomplished this turn and was facing the living room, he stopped and looked up to survey us watching him. He couldn't have been surprised to see Elena and Lou there, but I was apparently one more than he'd counted on. "Well, Elena," he said with a small eloquent snort and a lift of his chin, "you called out the whole fire department."

A suggestion of a smile was playing across his cheekbones, but I think my presence at this moment really didn't please him. Edmund was proud, and wanted no publicity for his disabilities. Even before he'd completed the descent of the stairs and settled into his accustomed chair, he told me brusquely that the case I'd made a couple of days before for another movie he hadn't liked was "rubbish." He was obviously glad though to find that Lou hadn't left, because after Lou had gone downstairs he'd identified him as the local doctor he'd heard about who'd pursued Semitic studies with the mythical Harry Wolfson at Harvard before studying medicine and who still knew some Hebrew. Edmund had published his early work on the Dead Sea Scrolls in 1955, but the book was not to appear until 1969 and his interest in Hebrew, which he'd begun to study ten years before in Princeton, was still active.

He therefore began to question Lou in the ruthless probing fashion for which he was infamous. The objects of these assaults could sometimes be made uncomfortable or even angry by them because they were so impersonal. He was after information, and the person who possessed the information was at that moment of little other interest to him. Lou, however, perhaps because he worked in a service profession anyway, was glad enough to share his knowledge. Edmund found out what he could, and after a while the conversation broadened. Reconciled to my presence by then, he drew me into it also. He seemed refreshed and hungry for intellectual conversation — with the hunger, I felt, of someone who a few hours earlier thought this pleasure had been abruptly terminated. When Lou and I finally left around 4:00 A.M., we had to make a forced departure. Edmund was prepared to go on talking for a long time, and he couldn't or wouldn't understand why we wished to leave. I can't remember this for certain, but I'd be surprised if he didn't say that Elena would be happy to make breakfast for us.

This incident strongly informs all of the few images I have of the last ten years of Edmund's life. After he and Elena left Cambridge and were living mostly in Wellfleet, we saw them only intermittently. But the incident is also, I believe, accurately emblematic of what that last decade was like for Edmund. I remember particularly three meetings in that time. One was in Boston, at the Ritz, a place he had long favored. The four of us were in the bar talking happily and indiscreetly about various friends and non-friends when a woman walked over to the table next to ours and sat down. Edmund instantly warned us, in French, to be silent, and when after a short time she got up and walked to another part of the room, he told us that he'd recognized her as a gossip columnist for one of the Boston papers who, in the old days, would not have been allowed to come into the bar. As his health and his mobility continued to deteriorate, however, Edmund came to Boston less often, and we were more likely to see him if we drove to Wellfleet—which I wish we'd done more often. On one of the few visits we did make, his legs were good enough to allow him to walk slowly with the aid of a stick. It was a fine day, and as we circled one of the nearby ponds, he halted to rest and indicated a line across the water with his stick. "The first time I saw Elena," he said, "she was swimming that way across the pond. You can't imagine how beautiful she was."

I could imagine it, for she was still beautiful, but I could now also imagine the affect of her beauty as I was frequently able to imagine the affect of Edmund's past as he talked about it. That day, too, he sang, or rather intoned, songs from musicals of the thirties and forties and, again reluctant to let us leave, came out onto the front porch of the beautiful, light-drenched Wellfleet house as we were going to delay us with one or two last songs.

But the final time we visited him in Wellfleet he wasn't certain he wanted to see us at all. That must have been in the winter or early spring of 1972. At any event, it wasn't long before his death. He'd been hospitalized for a mild coronary but had discharged himself from the hospital against medical advice to go to a circus, taken a fall, and badly injured his back. Ruefully, I thought, but also to keep the record straight, Elena told us that this mishap had not been necessary. Edmund could walk only with a walker now, and had sufficient difficulty with his arms and hands as well to make eating a meal a clumsy and uncertain process. He wouldn't, out of pride, join us in the dining room for the delicious lunch Elena had prepared, but ate by himself from a tray in the library, and he was distinctly cool at first when we went into the library to join him after lunch. When I began to talk about what I'd been reading in the past several weeks, though, his mood changed—changed so much that when we judged it was time to leave if we were not to overtire him, he protested our departure with an urgency in which I read, I think accurately, his knowledge that we were not going to talk together again.

Whether accurately or not I can't be certain, of course, but I see Edmund's anger in these last years of his life as never diffuse or blind, but directed as the blast of a jet engine to keep him in whatever motion was still possible on his true trajectory. And I hang onto my images of that final decade as vitally instructive even though I neither think of it as enviable nor see any ready, literal way to translate it to the needs of my own very different life.

EILEEN SIMPSON

Courier for Jacques Lacan

In 1962, when I went to live abroad, Jacques Lacan had little international reputation, so it was not surprising that I had not heard of him. But three years later, when I began work on an article for the *American Journal of Psychotherapy* about the psychoanalytic milieu in Paris, it became clear that while he was also not known to the general public, he was already a highly controversial figure in the city's small, intense, and incestuously close circle of analysts and intellectuals. In 1963, he had been expelled from the International Psychoanalytic Association for misconduct in both his professional and private life. While in exile, he plotted his return to a position of power, and a year later established the Ecole freudienne de Paris. Such was the force of his personality that before long he attracted a goodly number of disciples to join him on Elba.

It was during a period of relative calm in his extremely turbulent life that I interviewed him. Wishing to be as well prepared for the meeting as possible, I delayed calling for an appointment until I had talked to the heads of the other two analytic groups (who were reluctant to discuss him except in the most circumspect way) and thirty or so junior analysts and students (who were more than willing to share the gossip that circulated about the man they referred to as "*l'enfant terrible*"). I wrote ahead, as I had done before the other interviews, explaining my purpose.

That Dr. Lacan, who was said to be contemptuous of Americans, might refuse to see me was not at all unlikely. So it was with a flutter of nervousness that I dialed his number. When he, himself, answered the phone, I was thrown off guard. Quickly—too quickly—I explained why I was calling and asked if he would grant me a few minutes of his time.

If all I wanted was "a few minutes," he said testily, I could not possibly be serious about my investigation. Was my interest so superficial that I thought a few minutes would suffice? Did I know *who he was*?

It occurred to me that as I had heard the gossip about him, he had also

heard that I was going the rounds, and was nettled that I had waited so long
to contact him. My phrase had been ill-chosen, I admitted, since what I
really wanted was as much time as he could give me. I was living around
the corner on the rue de l'Université (not in Paris on the run), this project
my sole occupation.

Mollified, he said that while he had no time during the next ten days,
he would be free in two weeks. He would receive me at home, for lunch,
early enough to give us time to talk before he had to leave for an afternoon
class.

At noon, one day late in September, I pressed the button at 5, rue de Lille,
let myself into the courtyard, and climbed two flights of broad stone stairs.
A *bonne* in felt bedroom slippers responded to my ring. If the aromas (*pot
au feu*?) that floated from the kitchen could be trusted, she was a good cook.
"The Doctor," as he was called, practiced at home, as did the other analysts
I had interviewed. His apartment, like theirs, had many doors (always
closed) and hallways, and was large enough for the living and working
quarters to be quite separate. This apartment looked as if it had been furnished at the time its inhabitant began to practice, and had been left
unchanged — save for the addition of books and art objects — since then, so
that everything had a well-worn, comfortably shabby look. The *bonne* led
me to a small room and closed the door.

There was no place to sit down. While I was puzzling over how to interpret this oddity, my eyes were drawn to two studio photographs of a beautiful young woman that were set out on the table, as if they were being
studied in order to make a selection. I had heard that Lacan was married
to the actress Sylvia Bataille (who played the lead in Jean Renoir's *A Day
in the Country*). Was this one of their daughters? And, again, why no chair?

Fortunately, I didn't have to stand for long before the door was opened.
The man who entered shook my hand and trained his bespectacled eyes
on me. With one searing look, he had taken me in. He had learned what
he wanted to know, had made his diagnosis. I, on the other hand, was
trying to put together all I had heard about him — that he was a theoretician
who rivaled Freud, that he was *un cochon* (meaning, in this case, not only
'pig' but 'unprincipled person' as well), a charmer and womanizer, a
trouble-making paranoiac, a supremely gifted clinician, a genius. This
bundle of contradictions had a disproportionately large head, graying hair
brushed up from a high forehead, and heavy black eyebrows. If human ears

can be said to look alert, his did. Was I imagining it, or was there something Mephistophelian about his appearance?

As we went into lunch, he apologized for the simple meal we were about to have: he was on a *régime*. If this opening remark on so personal a note was a bid for sympathy, it was successful. When I said I was sorry he was not feeling well, he made a gesture of weariness. I could imagine, could I not, that the turmoil of recent years had taken its toll? Seated opposite me, his face framed by the window and, behind it, a dove-gray mat of the soft autumnal day, he looked careworn and considerably older than his sixty-four years.

The *bonne* brought a platter, put it on a trivet between us, and left us to serve ourselves. Did I know this Middle Eastern dish, Baba Ghannouj? my host asked, coaxing me to take a more generous portion. During the courses that followed (the obligatory four of a French lunch), which he urged on me but took little of himself, "The Old Man" (as he was also called) talked about his separation from the International Psychoanalytic Association. He suggested that he had left, rather than been expelled, because its leaders, like his former colleagues in France, had moved so far from Freud's teachings that they could hardly any longer be called Freudians. He, and he alone, was in the direct line.

Listening to French analysts, Freudians every one, talk about their relationship to the Master, I often imagined Freud as a Parisian papa who was attempting to assemble his large family for a Sunday drive in the family automobile. There was a noisy dispute as each child insisted that *he* was Papa's favorite and therefore should sit closest to him.

Lacan was saying that in the preceding twelve years there had been almost continual warring among his colleagues. The strife that had surrounded him, all of which would have been unnecessary if the others had been able to follow his theoretical development of Freud's texts, had drained his energy, all but broken his spirit. He was tired of these disputes. From now on he wanted to devote himself to educating the young, the cream of the arts and sciences students who attended his lectures at the Ecole normale supérieure. Others told him that he was having an enormous influence not only on analysts-in-training, but also on writers, Marxists, and the clergy.

Mention of the clergy led me to a question I wanted to ask of this Jesuit-educated analyst whose brother was a priest. It was thought in the United

States that one reason psychoanalysis had taken hold so slowly in France was the repressive influence of the Catholic church. Was this so?

The apostate almost permitted himself to smile. It was not that psychoanalysis had taken hold too slowly in France, but rather too quickly in the United States. This haste had led to chaotic fracturing into groups, to eclecticism, to deplorable shortcuts, to popularization. No, in France analysts had no conflict with the church, such as his colleagues in Spain and Italy reported. In Paris there were priest-analysts, and frequently when a vocation was in question, a seminarian was sent to him for consultation.

In December his lecture series at the Ecole normale would begin again. He would give me a card to present at the door for admission. After he had done so, we left the apartment together. Going down the stairs, he held the banister with one hand, and asked if he might have my arm as a support for the other. As we descended slowly, he said my husband and I must come to visit him in the country so we could talk in a more leisurely way. I said he must come to see us on the rue de l'Université. I knew his invitation was not serious. He knew mine was.

Six weeks later, when I telephoned to invite him, he said he would be delighted to join us for dinner. At the table were the Wests (Mary McCarthy and Jim), the Wylies (Laurence, on leave from Harvard, was Cultural Attaché at the American Embassy), a French writer and her husband. Having learned by what I hoped was delicate questioning that the guest of honor would be coming without his wife (from whom, it was said, he had been separated for some time), I invited as the extra woman an Indo-Chinese divorcée-about-town.

The last to arrive, Dr. Lacan entered the living room with a buoyant step. In a well-tailored dinner jacket, the man who so recently had looked seventy now looked fifty. His hair was less gray (a blue rinse at Carita's, gossip had it) and his somber expression had been replaced by one that was lively, even mischievous. There was no sign of a careful diet as he rollicked through the meal, accepting wine each time it was poured.

My husband, who had questioned the wisdom of my having lunch in the apartment of a man I had never met, a Frenchman, and one with an unsavory reputation, had been reassured by my report of the interview. If Lacan had his demonic side, the one he had presented to me had been benign, elderly, sad—the broken spirit, convalescent's appetite, signs of premature aging in the face, and need for assistance going down the stairs. I was no less astonished than Bob, as I told him later, at this rejuvenation. I felt as though I had seen Faust before and after the bargain was struck.

Lacan had a reputation for being either charming or outrageous in social life, depending on the situation. Which would he be tonight? During the early part of the meal, playing the engaging dinner companion, he asked lightly about how my article was going with the air of a fond professor indulging a favorite student. Yes, I could feel the charm. Within a few minutes of his turning to talk to Mary McCarthy, however, I observed a sharp change in his manner. As Mary quizzed him about Freud's study of Leonardo, I wondered how long it had been since anyone had challenged him as she was doing. Would he become irritable? Or, worse, commit the besetting sin of French intellectuals and attempt to patronize her? Sparks flew between them, but he listened judiciously to her criticisms and addressed them seriously (if, as she said later, unconvincingly). He joined the conversation I was having with Laurence Wylie and steered it to talk about Harvard. What he seemed most eager to know about was the caliber of the students there, how they compared with those at the *grandes écoles* in Paris. Remembering that I had said at lunch that I had lived in Princeton, he asked about the Gauss Seminars: who invited the speakers? how many attended? what was the level of the discussion?

After dinner, he talked French politics with Bob. Bob said that when the divorcée joined them in conversation, Lacan appreciated her décolletage. When it was time to leave, he gallantly offered to see her home.

It was not unusual in Paris for a guest to send flowers following a dinner party. The next morning when a delivery boy handed me Lacan's card and a box, I felt certain it would not contain a predictable selection. Enfolded in tissue paper was a single, exquisite orchid of a species I had never seen before.

In December, I went to the opening lecture at the Ecole normale. The lecture hall was filling up when I arrived. There were fifty or sixty in attendance. Many were of student age, others older; there were also a few women and five or six clerics. (Marxists were more difficult to spot, so I couldn't estimate their number.) There was a feeling of excitement in the air. Much hand-shaking. Animated conversation on all sides. At a certain moment conversation stopped abruptly. As the lecturer entered from the rear and walked down the right aisle, all eyes followed him. I can't swear that he was wearing a cape, but whatever his outer garment, he divested himself of it with a flourish.

Pad and pen at the ready for note-taking, I listened carefully. The subject was the unconscious. Or was it? I had the impression I was following, but after fifteen minutes I realized I had understood nothing. Lacan's prose style was so convoluted (where was that Cartesian clarity the French prized so highly?) that I had counted heavily on the lectures to help me to get a grip on his theories. After another half hour, I knew I was completely lost. As I looked around the room, it seemed to me that the audience was hypnotized. In Charcot's city, there was a doctor at the lectern who, had he been a clinician in a turn-of-the-century hospital, would have been famous for curing hysterics. The question I asked myself in each encounter with Lacan was, Would I trust this man with my unconscious?

At the end of the lecture, I confessed to the man seated next to me that I had not understood. Could he tell me what it had been about? My neighbor asked how long I had been attending these classes. "Your first time? I've been coming for six years and I still don't understand," he said. Why, then, had he continued for so long? "For the theater. The Doctor is better entertainment than Barrault at the Odéon." And then, making a gesture to take in the room, he added, "That's why we're all here."

After the second and third lectures, I questioned others. They, too, admitted to being mystified. Or they said they came for the amusement to be had from Lacan's verbal gymnastics — the puns, paradoxes, and epigrams. There were others undoubtedly, especially analysts-in-training, who, having familiarized themselves with the special vocabulary and become habituated to the style, were able to follow the labyrinthine theorizing, and followed it with excitement. They belonged to that race of Parisian intellectuals who, as Jane Kramer said in the *New Yorker*, "behave as though thinking is a swashbuckling and erotic art."

During the seventies, which have been called "the glory days of Lacanism," whenever I returned to Paris for a visit, I tried to catch up on what was going on. An American friend of mine who was in treatment with The Doctor described some of his sessions. One of the early criticisms of the way Lacan conducted his practice had been aimed at his innovation of shortening the hour to twenty or so minutes. By the time my friend Donald was seeing him, the short session had become what I thought of as the short-short. Donald reported that after an introductory period of some weeks at full time, he had arrived one day bursting to report a dream. At the end of his recital, he had been dismissed with the injunction to go away and work on it on his own.

Five minutes after the session had begun, Donald was out on the street. He walked in a daze, turned into a cul-de-sac, and found himself in front of the church of St. Thomas d'Acquin (a block away from 5, rue de Lille). An apostate (like his analyst), he entered and, seated in a rear pew, struggled to understand the riches his unconscious had tossed up the previous night. He expressed no resentment at having paid the full fee (in cash) and said he would pass on to Lacan my suggestion that he use the church as an annex, a kind of study hall for disoriented patients who reeled out of his office and were looking for a place to do their homework.

Junior analysts I questioned during these years said there had been a radical change in Lacan's attitude toward the United States. From having been highly critical of this country in the sixties, he had become convinced that Americans would be more open to his writings than his countrymen. What I suspected was that even in 1965 he had been looking toward the New World for a larger audience than France could provide him with. I remembered that shortly before I left Paris for New York, he had telephoned me. He had a great favor to ask, he said. A reporter from *Time* had requested an interview, but this man didn't seem to know *who he was*. Would I see the reporter before he did, explain to my compatriot? . . . It was important. . . . He would be most grateful.

Lacan saw me as a courier. I would draw an attractive picture of him in my article. I would talk to the people at Princeton about his giving a Gauss Seminar (which I did) and perhaps even mention him to *his* old analyst, Dr. Loewenstein (which I didn't). I would talk to the reporter from *Time* ("Who does this character Lacan think he is anyway?"), explain that even if the reporter didn't understand Lacan's importance as a thinker, he was worth paying attention to because he was on his way to becoming a media star.

Only a few years later, during the student revolution of 1968, he did become a star in France. And, as he suspected, America was indeed hospitable to his ideas, although just how hospitable I don't think he could have predicted. Whenever I pick up a magazine of film criticism these days, or hear students use his vocabulary as they "think Lacan," I imagine how gratified he would be. Or would he? I can also imagine the irritation in his voice as he protested, "No, no, no." And then added — echoing the physicist Wolfgang Pauli's astringent remark made in another context —"No, that is not even wrong."

JOHN HOLLANDER

Remembering Auden

I am reticent about writing of my first meeting with W. H. Auden because of my own peculiarly bad memory for things said on particular occasions, and, more interestingly, because of some of his own implicit injunctions. I can almost hear him propounding them in his characteristic mode of semi-private declamation: (1) There should be no gossip in or for print and (2) when you write of something or someone don't talk about yourself. On an occasion like this I could only wish to be — as was once said of the author of a celebrated *New Yorker* profile —"an idiot with total recall." Not having anything like that kind of recall, it is hard to stay invisible. Besides, I was then at such an awkward age — not yet eighteen and an uneducated sophomore in college — that I was totally unable to ask him the questions that, on so many occasions since, I have wished I could have put to him as he was then (at the age of forty, seventeen years younger than I am now). And yet Auden was the poet whose cadences had become so much an undersong in my own verse that, ten years after that first meeting, I still had to rewrite in proof many lines of my first book of poems, to expunge embarrassingly blatant echoes of his voice.

That "voice" is a trope in disfavor in fashionably advanced academic critical circles today is of little matter for serious poetry. Before I ever met him, I had (as Hazlitt put it) "a sound in my ears — it was the voice of Fancy; I had a light before me — it was the face of Poetry." The sound had come from the pages of Auden's poetry: in my freshman year at Columbia I had bought a copy of the 1945 *Collected Poems*, still in its dark-green binding — a slimmer volume than subsequent printings produced because of the thin, gray wartime paper. In the first semester of my freshman year I remember thinking of Robinson Jeffers as a favorite contemporary poet, but during the remainder of that year I began to read Auden, Yeats, and Stevens, puzzling them out by myself. And while I had committed to memory more lines of Eliot, Pound, and these three other poets than I had of Keats,

Shelley, or Wordsworth, it was Auden's *voice* that I fancied I heard coming off the page at me.

The poems I knew best then were an odd assortment of light pieces and portions of *The Sea and the Mirror*. But there were others, too, including "Heavy Date," "O, Where Are You Going?," "Musée des Beaux-Arts," and "September 1, 1939," of course, with its figure of contingent hope, the "ironic points of light"—which spoke at once to my New Yorker's native landscape and my moviegoer's familiarity with its black-and-white transformations in night background shots. (Eventually Auden repudiated "September 1, 1939." "I won't let you reprint it," he said to me years later, "because, you know, it's bogus.") Then, too, there were poems like "The Maze" and "Law Like Love," the ballads, and the elegies for Freud and Yeats — all these spoke to me in the imagined tones of the voice of a teacher. My only other teacher-at-a-distance had been George Bernard Shaw, whom I had started reading in elementary school. Shaw, Auden, and, later on, Orwell all served at various times as moral teachers for me, but Auden was the only one I ever knew. On first meeting him I seem now to have heard his imagined voice and his actual one, which I came to know so well in later years, blended indefinably.

The increasingly famous Face was another matter. Before reading a word of him, I remember seeing his photograph accompanying a lead review of the *Collected Poems* in either the *New York Times Book Review* or the *Saturday Review of Literature*. I first read then, in 1945, about this important younger poet. I had heard his name before only in some joking light verse (by Morris Bishop, I believe, with a dreadful pun which delighted me at fourteen, something about "Whether we ought or whether we Auden"), but when I asked for an explanation I was told only that his was the name of a clever modern poet. I am shocked now by the actual pictures of him taken in those years, partially because my memory is primarily of that later Face ("He's been years building it up," a common friend said years later), with its remarkable systems of wrinkles, palimpsestically overlaid on what I saw but cannot now actually remember.

In any event, my first glimpses of the poet himself had been prepared for by a good deal of adulation, and somewhat less knowledge, of the man and the work. I had known that he was then living at 7 Cornelia Street, a stone's throw from the building in Greenwich Village which housed the printers of the *Columbia Spectator*, for which I had written a good deal

of news and feature copy as a freshman, and which I frequently had to put
to bed downtown late at night. (The abode of e. e. cummings on Patchin
Place was also known to me and some friends, and occasionally haunted
for ten minutes or so in the hopes of catching a Glimpse.) But I had never
seen or heard Auden, even publicly, until the late winter of 1947, when I
was in my second year at Columbia.

He was then appearing at Barnard College to teach a course under Ursula
Niebuhr's auspices called "The Quest in Ancient and Modern Literature."
A young lady I was pursuing at the time was taking it, and various Quests
of my own—for the poet's voice and face, for a sip of Castalian water, for
the lady's company and (I hoped) person—all converged on the lecture
room. I attended a few of those sessions, daunted by the reading list (from
Gilgamesh—this was the first I had heard of it—through Kafka's *The
Castle*) and fascinated by the originality of the agenda. I had loved since
childhood "The Hunting of the Snark" and Edward Lear's "The Jumblies,"
but to hear this somewhat high-pitched and unresonant voice bracketing
these with *Moby-Dick* in a mode of romantic Argonautica was electrifying.
(Some of his observations would resurface later on in the lectures he gave
at the University of Virginia, which became that unique and wonderful
little book called *The Enchafèd Flood*.) But not being officially enrolled in
the course, I was far too shy to approach the speaker after class.

The first occasion at which we actually met was on an evening in May
of that year, at a dinner celebrating the annual Boar's Head Poetry Prizes
at Columbia, newly instituted after World War II. Columbia under-
graduates competed for first and second prizes of one hundred dollars and
fifty dollars, if I remember correctly (a considerable sum in those days—
thirty dollars was a month's rent in a comfortable, safe, Lower East Side
cold-water flat). The money came from funds given to the then-moribund
literary society called Philoexian; it originally endowed a grand prize for
a patriotic oration, to consist of a plaster cast of Houdon's bust of George
Washington, with its huge jaws. The *Columbia Review* sought to use these
funds for a poetry contest that had been held before the war, accompanied
by a reading and an Honored Guest. Due to the efforts of the business manager, a nascent lawyer, we contrived to have the income of the patriotic bust
fund diverted to the service of Calliope. (I must add that, a very few years
later, the contest for the patriotic oration was gravely and frivolously reintroduced for a year, the prize being won with a ringing encomium of Henry
James's essay on Hawthorne—what could be more *American*?—by the pre-

cociously sophisticated Robert Gottlieb.) There were sufficiently few con-
testants in 1947 (in those decent days of *poeta fit, non nascitur,* fewer young
persons believed themselves to be bards than do today's multitudes) to
allow for all of them to read one or two poems after the prizewinners had
been celebrated and the Honored Guest heard from.

His presence on Morningside Heights earlier that spring allowed us to
think of asking Auden, and, to our delight, he agreed to come uptown and
to sing for what was only his supper (he asked to read through the student
poems and to make a few comments at the reading). As the precocious but
naive editor of the *Columbia Review* that year (the unstaffed but college-
funded quarterly had fallen to me, a sophomore, by default), I got to plan
the evening, arrange the dinner at the Faculty Club, and attend it *ex officio,*
for my wretched poems had not placed at all in the competition. The
prizewinners were a returned World War II pilot named Coman Leaven-
worth, who had written some amazingly polished and (I now see) very
Audenesque poems, and Allen Ginsberg, whose entry was a pastiche of
Marvell's "The Garden." They, the editors, and the judges of the contest —
that year they were Lionel Trilling and the formidable and locally fabulous
Andrew Chiappe — assembled for dinner, before the reading, with Auden.

I waited for him by the door. I noticed that he was wearing carpet slippers
and felt there to be something peculiar about this: were his feet bad? or
temporarily injured? or had he forgotten his shoes in a rush to get here on
time? Two summers before, when working as an office boy at the *New
Yorker,* I had had to pick up some proofs from the celebrated cartoonist
Peter Arno at his Park Avenue apartment at two in the afternoon: he came
to the door in pyjamas and dressing gown, which seemed marvelously
louche to me at the time, and there was *something* about those carpet
slippers. There was also something resonant about his first words after the
perfunctory greetings. In response to a waiter who appeared with a request
for a drink order, he said — and I can still hear the sound of his voice, though
I can scarcely remember what he sounded like in those lectures at
Barnard —"I'll have an old fashioned, please." Of this, too, I wondered at
the possible significance (barely of drinking age, I had only a visionary tax-
onomy of mixed drinks). Was there something about this choice of drink
that I didn't know? Was its name self-descriptive of its social style? Or was
it preferred in the literary circles, mysteriously both advanced and established, in which I supposed the poet to move?

Of the early dinner (in those days the Columbia Faculty Club was not noted for its cuisine, although for a shy sophomore it was a low-voltage thrill to be eating there at all), I can remember nothing, and of the discourse, very little. Considering the conversation of other guests and what they must have said, this vacancy of memory is all a bit shocking and, to me, now, terribly disappointing. It was in all innocence that, in my youth, I could never keep a journal — it seemed too self-important, and was indeed too demanding of a consistency of attention I didn't possess. And so I was rather like a child being taken to see various wonders of a minor world — the gardens of Castle Rubbish, the Great Memorial Museum, the cute-as-a-button one-ring circus — and remembering not the famous and canonical sights but only the train ride, the pattern of tiles on the floor of the men's room, the discovered delights of a complex of interconnected rooms, things no grown-up would notice. So with the old fashioned, and the sound of the voice. I was lost in an inner museum of my own, trying to put together the particular cadences, the variations of pitch, the speeding up and slowing down of the phrases in conversation that sounded so different from the imperfectly enunciated and sometimes swallowed reading of his Barnard lectures (James Merrill conjures these up marvelously on the pages of *The Changing Light at Sandover*) with the fictive inner voice I had heard speaking his poems to me from the page. But it was the sound of that voice — its famously wide range of pitch, its periodic slowing of articulation, its bursts of speed at what even then were homiletic moments (and here the speaker became a strange combination of tutor, nanny, and co-conspirator) — that marked his speech, even as the "we" of many of his poems compounded the usage of the editorial desk, the royal proclamation, the pulpit, and the nursery.

I do remember his talking at the reading of the importance of young poets' using models well to discover their own voices, and, as always, of the significance of form. The audience in the well-filled room wanted, I think, to hear more from him about crisis theology and Marxism, about "private faces in public places"—as he put it in the epigraph to *The Orators* — and about the relation of criticism to poetry. Allen Ginsberg, who had written a brief essay on *The Sea and the Mirror* for our magazine the previous spring, was concerned with that poem in particular; but what fascinated me was the introduction Auden gave to the value of difficulty — not in construing but in constructing, in "making," to invoke his own later triad, rather than merely in knowing and judging. He may have invoked

Paul Valéry then, as I know he did in a conversation fourteen years later: "I agree with Valéry when he says a poet is a person whose imagination is stimulated by arbitrary rules. He meant that if it is not stimulated but is insulted by them, he'd better write prose." But I had been bottle-fed (by the magical attentions of Brooks and Warren's textbook, *Understanding Poetry*, which I had read while in high school) on the notion of formal strictures holding in check passionate thoughts and cognitively charged passions, and this other notion filled me with some wonder.

I think, too, that this was the first occasion on which I heard him talk of the elements of problem-solving and of unriddling that poetry and crossword puzzles have in common. It was certainly the scene of my being introduced to the idea that playing with words, loving them and their apparent relations, characters, and habits, was more essential to the birth of poetry than lofty thoughts, aesthetic programs (particularly radically modernist ones), or even being enamored of Eros — and enamored I was at that time. (Not yet eighteen, yet spiritually fuzzy around the edges, I described myself — recording my grim joke in a notebook — as "Half in death with easeful love.") I couldn't easily believe that the Muse was made of language rather than of a particular absent body, and could be a stern monitor of one's behavior in times of intellectual crisis (which I had heard about in relation to Auden, but didn't know enough about modern theology even to grasp weakly). But coming over the years to understand how and in what ways this was true has been an important side road on the map of my life as a writer, and wonder at the notion started that evening. Fourteen years later, in 1961, in the visionary clutter of the St. Mark's Place apartment that was his last dwelling in New York City, he summed this matter up resonantly, full of overtones of Lichtenberg, Karl Kraus, and some of his other favorite aphorists: "A poet is someone who uses a language he didn't create, which has its own wonderful property. And one is in the position — rather of, well — it's like a marriage bed where the poet speaks as the husband and the language is the wife who bears the child. And naturally, she has a lot to say in what is said." (I can record this, not from an incredible lapse of my usual amnesia, but from notes taken at the time for a *Paris Review* interview which never crystallized.)

I can also remember that he mentioned, in a brief discussion that followed the reading and his public remarks, that he had been working on a new poem (I now estimate that it had been finished some time in

February). He talked primarily of its formal mode of alliterative verse, with which I was slightly familiar from having read parts of *Piers Plowman* for a survey course in English literature. That new poem was *The Age of Anxiety*, which I got to read when it was published that summer. It happened that I was in Denver on my way across the country, staying briefly with Allen Ginsberg, who told me of the poem's appearance; I went with him to a bookstore and bought a copy (it's inscribed "July 10, 1947"). We sat outdoors and read parts of it aloud, and I remember Allen maintaining that the "lost dad, / Our colossal father" in the section called "The Dirge" must be Roosevelt. Be that as may be, I cannot remember Wystan Auden saying anything much to me on that night in May, nor, indeed, a few weeks later when he also came to Columbia to read "Music Is International" as the Phi Beta Kappa poem that year.

In fact, I would not see him again for five years — five years during which I got to know most of his work rather well, had his companion Chester Kallman pointed out to me at the San Remo bar, became acquainted with his friend Alan Ansen, read "In Praise of Limestone" in *Horizon*, graduated from college, went abroad, and returned to graduate school at Indiana University. In Bloomington, in the winter of 1952–53, I finally got to meet and talk with him. He had given a well-attended reading in a rather grand hall and was staying the night at the student union building, a totally dry establishment on a totally dry campus. This time I did go backstage, blessed with a bit more assurance, and, presuming on the occasion he must have forgotten and on the name of a common acquaintance or two, I secured a meeting at breakfast the next morning, in a large student cafeteria with jukeboxes going even at that time of day. He complained of being given fruit punch the night before, and I had to explain the unavailability of liquor. But he talked of many things during that hour and a half, and by then I knew much more of what he, I myself, and the matter of poetry all were, so that the occasion was less awesome but far more satisfactory than my first meeting with him had been.

This was the first time at which he said certain things that he would reiterate over the years that I knew him. On hearing that I was studying for a Ph.D. and working in the Renaissance, he made it clear that he disapproved of teaching "creative writing." Praising colleges and universities as patrons of writers, he insisted that the writers should not agree to have anything to do with teaching contemporary literature. "They should teach the eighteenth century or something," he said. Years later he would confess that even in teaching a historical body of literature, he would prefer not to assign papers to the students, but rather have them write stylistic pastiches of the poems, plays, or novels in question, arguing that such would constitute a far better test of what they had been able to apprehend. I don't know if he ever actually did this, however. Questions of poetry and science came up, and he was interested to learn that my father was a physiologist, remarking that his father had been a doctor and that he had grown up in a house where — as he put it some years later, I remember —"science and literature were both humanities." When in 1962 he did meet my father at a party, he spent a good deal of time talking with him, and would inquire about him subsequently. And in the days, a few years after, when my father was dying, I found that Wystan Auden was the one person I could talk to of my agitation about medical and familial pretense and euphemism: he told me then of how he had been able to discuss his own father's dying with him, as I had not been able to do.

He also spoke then of the upcoming first performance at the Metropolitan Opera of *The Rake's Progress,* two and a half years after its world premiere in Venice, and of how he preferred singers to American actors for speaking verse in the theater. I remember very well his lack of interest in talking about his early plays, and his extremely resonant remark about the difference between writing for composers and for silent readers, as poets today usually do. "The success in writing for music," he said, "consists in how well what you write will get the composer to compose." This led to matters of poetic impersonality more generally, and his saying that he thought poets ought, particularly when young, to look like everyone else — something which, I did not add at the time, I had, unhappily, always failed to do. I was just beginning to understand in those days how the rhetoric of personal distancing that was so personal a matter for T. S. Eliot had become something of a modernist principle. But in any case, these were the days of America's introduction to the elaborately rhapsodic public performances of Dylan Thomas, and his cautioning against the public role of the *poète maudit* thus had more than antiquarian interest.

I could never, in those days, think of myself as a poet (nor, indeed, would I allow myself to, or to accept the word as designation, until I was thirty-five and had published three books of poems). If one was serious, one had the good sense and taste not to make such a claim. But I had recently published three prose poems in something grander than a campus journal – the *New Directions* annual, which also contained prose poems by my slightly older contemporaries Allen Ginsberg and John Ashbery (Ashbery's were the good ones) – which may have helped me in some part to begin to entertain the possibility, during this conversation, of my having some future literary legitimacy. But perhaps it was only the fact of the informality of the breakfast. (How much less alarming now were the carpet slippers in which he again appeared!) I was the kind of fan, I fear, that I would myself today pray silently for the patience to deal with; Auden's generosity with his time was nothing I could understand then. Nor could I begin to conceive of how I was more deeply and mysteriously affected by these early encounters with Auden than with later ones which might at first appear to be more significant: my correspondence with him over his having taken my first book of verse for the Yale Series of Younger Poets (because I so deeply admired some of his previous selections, this was particularly moving for me); the occasion, beautifully arranged by our common friend William Meredith, at which I was reintroduced, somewhat more *au pair*, after my book had appeared; and all the other occasions over the subsequent years, the meetings in New York, New Haven (where I then taught), New York again.

Only the very last time I saw Auden, visiting him and Chester Kallman in Kirchstetten with my wife and young daughters, on the way to spend a week in Vienna, is now as resonant. Even in that last, somewhat ill, somewhat cranky stage of his life his generosity toward my children is memorable. He asked all in the room – and them particularly – to try to recall the earliest public event they remembered, mentioning that in his case it was hearing of the *Titanic* disaster. (For my older daughter, it was John Kennedy's assassination; for her sister, four years younger, it was the murder of his brother; for me, it was actually seeing the *Morro Castle* burning off the New Jersey shore.) It was a sunny July day; we arrived by car, amused and delighted to see that the street he lived on, Hinterholz, had been renamed Audenstrasse. He had recently returned from reading at a Poetry International Festival in London, where he had had an amusing and slightly awkward encounter with Allen Ginsberg; his mentioning this caused me to remind him of the original occasion at the Boar's Head Poetry Reading when we had first met, and, indeed, of the importance of his presence in New York during the following fifteen years for so many poets of my generation — not just to those of us who had been at Columbia, including Richard Howard, Daniel Hoffman, and Louis Simpson, but James Merrill and John Ashbery as well. I had, of course, not the slightest notion that I would never see him again, that he would die two months later, at the same age as my father.

A short time ago, I called my daughter, who is now a graduate student in California, to talk about the occasion. I asked her what she particularly remembered. She said it was a picture of Yeats on the wall, which she recognized, and Chester Kallman's splendid lunch, at which she had encountered polenta for the first time. This was her "I'll have an old fashioned, please." It was a far more emblematic token than mine.

Maugham

*Like Semele who longed to see God and was wrapped in fire which
consumed her, so I longed for fame and was destroyed by it.*
— Peter Ackroyd, *The Last Testament of Oscar Wilde*

My first book was accepted by Heinemann in London on 30 October 1953.
I know because the date is in a letter from Somerset Maugham, inviting
me to lunch in his suite at the Dorchester at one o'clock. I still have the letter
and every two or three years I have to look at it again and bring back the
day, like a necessary cold shower.

He asked me to bring Angus Wilson, now Sir Angus Wilson, England's
most prestigious living writer. I admired Wilson beyond any other postwar
English writer. He was, and is, a mentor to me. His rare combination of
social awareness and style was a goal I only hoped for. In 1953, he was at
the beginning of his critical success — praise beyond my own wildest
dreams. I was a young writer whose fiction had not yet been published,
and who, having made a vow not to take a "regular" job until I had bought
myself time to write, made a precarious living writing fashion and "cultural" journalism. Maugham, then in his eightieth year, was as heavy with
honors and fortune as any writer in the world.

I remember thinking when I read the Heinemann letter how auspicious
it was, after ten years of apprenticeship, to celebrate with those two, the
newest and the most established, that day of all days. It seemed to be magic,
a dream membership in a faraway circle of acceptance and understanding.
I took some pride in going, as usual, to the British Museum to work on
my current book, which was *O Beulah Land*. I told myself that I had not
let ten years of rejection stop me, and I certainly was not going to let acceptance do it. I think I saw acceptance then as some great gold curtain parting,
like the beginning announcement of the Saturday afternoon opera broad-
casts from the old Met that I had listened to when I was growing up.

I had first met Somerset Maugham in early October; I had gone in fear and trembling to interview him at the Dorchester Hotel in London with two layouts of photographs for *Look* magazine taken when he was making a speech in America. The article was to celebrate his eightieth birthday. My assignment was to ask him for remarks that would act as captions.

I wore, I remember, low-heeled shoes. He was a short man and I had been warned that he was oversensitive, sarcastic, unkind. He looked the part — the creased, bitter, saurian face, the down-turned mouth of Graham Sutherland's portrait and the cold photograph by Karsh. I had studied them both and whatever else I could find, and I looked forward to the afternoon with a mixture of excitement and dread. I had been told that he had an appalling stammer, which terrified me because I, too, stammer when I am tired or when I am with another stammerer. I had a sick vision of us gobbling and gasping at each other. I stood in the lobby of the Dorchester and my voice shook when I asked to be announced.

Mr. Maugham's secretary, Alan Searle, answered the door and told me that Mr. Maugham was still taking his nap. He apologized and left me to wait and tremble. I can still see the room, the two soft sofas set on either side of a dead fireplace in a parody of a country house living room, the muted colors of expensive cloth, the heavy silk curtains, the reproductions of antiques, the soundless carpet. I began to relax. Nothing makes me feel more secure than the rich anonymity of a luxury hotel room. I was at that point living in a communal house with bare floors in Chelsea where color covered poverty, and visual wit emptiness. I found such dumb pastel luxury, even through the nervousness, a comfort.

Mr. Maugham came and stood for a second in the door. He was small, shy, and plump. He was dressed in old tweeds with patches at the elbows. The down-turned lines by his mouth were gone. He was smiling. He called me "my dear," and not once in the three hours that followed did he stammer. Now I must find his voice, or his voice for that day, and this is the way I remember it.

He said, "My dear, I know why you're here," as if we had met in Aladdin's cave, which, for me, we had, there on that cozy warm late afternoon in London with the early evening lowering outside. "Now, let me see the layouts. We can get these out of the way." He sat down on one of the sofas with the layouts on a coffee table in front of him. There were two full pages, and he went through them as if he were reading captions already there.

"Let's see now. What on earth would I have been saying when I looked like that? Something about America, I think. They (the mysterious *they*) always like for me to say something about America. Youamericans"— that single English word for us —"are so self-conscious, my dear."

So he went through picture after picture. "Something about France. They always like something about France . . . and sex . . . and changes in the world. . . ." When he had finished he handed the layouts to me and lounged back on the sofa. I could hear the tea cart rumbling along the hall outside. The whole process, including the arrival of tea, had taken less than half an hour. When that cozy rite was done and the waiter had left, he said with a sigh, as if he had been doing the washing, "Now that's done, my dear. We can talk. Tell me about yourself."

What could I tell him? That I had worked for fashion magazines? That I had been in the war? That I was working every day in the Reading Room of the British Museum on a novel that I had no hope for, since novels about history were denigrated as unfashionable? My other two unpublished novels? My six unproduced plays? No, nothing to tell. He didn't wait for me to tell him nothing.

"I love my yearly visit to London," he said for a beginning, and then he went on for most of the afternoon, as the night came down outside. He was anecdotal, entertaining, warm, and, dare I say, sweet—but he really was, the man with the reputation of a snapping turtle. I was embarrassed at staying so long, but he charmed me into staying. I realize as I write, so many years later, that Alan Searle had gone out and that Mr. Maugham did not want to be left alone. He was old. He had a new and very willing ear, unjudging and young. I was baby-sitting.

I forgot that it was an "interview" and simply asked questions gleaned from the homework I had done. I wanted to know why, with all the successful plays that he had written, he had let someone else write the most memorable, *Rain*. He was a conjurer. We were not in London in the dim afternoon. We were in Hollywood in 1920: white Spanish houses, sand, palms, sunshine, Keystone Cops, and Pearl White. He sat one evening, he said, on the patio of the Garden of Allah, the legendary cluster of cottages where visiting writers stayed in the early days of silent Hollywood.

"John Colton," he said, "was a friend of mine who was staying there, too. He came out and sat down beside me, and told me that he had not slept for several nights. He looked terrible, dark circles and all. I had the proofs of a book of short stories that had just come in the mail for me. I threw it to him, and said, 'Here, these will put you to sleep.'

"The next morning he came out on the patio again. He looked worse. 'Dammit, Willy, I haven't slept a wink,' he told me. 'Why haven't you made a play of that story, Sadie Thompson?' Now, you must understand that I of all people knew what a play was. After all, I had three hit plays running in London at the same time. I told him so. He asked me if he could try. I said, 'Of course, but you're wasting your time.'

"When the play he called *Rain* opened in Boston you could have bought it for five thousand dollars. It ran for six years and killed the loveliest actress I have ever known, Jeanne Eagels. I saw her one evening play a glorious performance, and when she came offstage she fainted. She had been playing with a safety pin stabbing her in the side, and when we undressed her, the blood had nearly soaked through her clothes."

Sometimes he didn't wait for me to ask a question. "I know what you're going to ask. I know you're here because I'm eighty next week. Changes in the world, they always ask about changes in the world." He jumped up. "Now I know you expect me to talk about wars, and all that. But you forget that I was trained as a doctor. No. Not war. *The modern contraceptive.* That's what has changed the world. In the old days"— he began to play an imaginary game of tennis around the room —"we lobbed the ball gently over the net so the lady we were playing with could hobble over gracefully and lob it back. Now!" His face changed. He crouched down. "We stand at back center court and fight for our lives!"

I did get a question in then. I asked him what it felt like to publish his first book in 1897, the same year the greats like Henry James, Joseph Conrad, H. G. Wells, and Rudyard Kipling were bringing out some of their most famous novels.

"Oh, were they?" he said vaguely. "My dear, we weren't paying any attention to *them.* We were reading George Meredith. He was our god. We all learned from him. Nobody reads Meredith now. You can tell from the bad prose. Conrad? James? Oh come, come, who were they? It was Meredith. Have you read him?" I was afraid to say no. "I can see you haven't. Read him. You read Meredith."

He said, "You know, one of my pleasures when I come on my visit to London is to meet some of the new writers. Now, there is a young man called Angus Wilson. I would love to meet him. Do you know him?"

I was able to tell him with some just pride that I saw Angus Wilson every day. He was still working in the Reading Room, and writing at night and on weekends. I knew he was working on a novel. I was even so bemused by the afternoon's warmth that I thought it possible to suggest that I give them both dinner.

"My dear, that is kind. But you see, I don't really like to go out at night, and I think it best if you brought Mr. Wilson here for luncheon. Now where would I write to invite him?"

I'm afraid that the next morning I gushed: "Everybody is wrong about Mr. Maugham. He's as benign as Santa Claus. He wants to meet you. I told him you were working very hard on a book but that you might."

"I wouldn't miss it for the world," Angus Wilson said, with less ecstasy and more irony.

Even in the taxi to the Dorchester that day, I babbled on about the magic coincidence of my book being accepted on such a day, and about what a surprise Mr. Maugham was going to be to him. There were no more fears when I called Alan Searle and told him we were there.

Maugham stood a few feet behind Alan Searle, framed by the room. He was his portrait and his reputation. He wore another face — reptilian, defensive, cold. His clothes were *de rigueur* for bankers in the city: the black jacket, the pinstriped trousers, the dead-white collar, the black tie with daring faint stripes. Outside of shaking hands, he never spoke to me but twice in the next two terrible hours. I had brought Angus Wilson into a literary lion's den. I was a Chinese go-between, nothing else. We all sat down on the two sofas. Searle poured martinis from a pitcher.

I realized, of course, what had happened. Angus Wilson was a rival and a threat. I had not been. I had been an interlude, probably forgotten. Wilson was, for that day, all the enemies that paranoid man had had to contend with during his later writing life. Unfair? Of course it was unfair. Wilson was and is the most generous critic and writer in England, more helpful to the young than Maugham ever thought of being, a fine stylist, a natural teacher. I can still hear his voice as, in casual conversation at the Reading Room, he would give me clue after clue, generous and subtle and right. One was that genius can only be imitated, not learned from —"Study Stacy O'Maunier to learn to construct a short story," I hear him say. "Craft. That's what we can learn from other writers, not genius."

But that day, as a new contender in that arena I did not yet know, he had to fight. I hardly remember Maugham taking his eyes off him. Question after question. There was not a leading writer who had visited his house in Cap Ferrat that Maugham did not destroy. My idols and mentors fell, one after another. He accused this one of drunkenness, that one of dirty habits, T. S. Eliot of stealing his books. Alan Searle and I just looked at each other and drank martinis.

At last I heard the lunch trolley being wheeled down the hall, and the waiter came in and set up a table in the room.

Maugham sat at its head, Searle at the foot, Wilson and I at either side. By the time lunch came Maugham was stammering so badly that I could see that part of the arrogant head-thrown-back look was his habitual attempt to recover his voice. He had one of the worst stammers I have ever heard, and, needless to say, I wouldn't have dared open my mouth had he given me a chance to.

Finally, though, he looked at me, from high above my face. "We're having p-p-p-p-partridge for lunch," he said. "Would you like i-i-i-ice cream or ch-ch-cheese to follow?"

Very very carefully, I said, "Cheese."

He put his nose very close to Wilson's face, and, a little ominously, he asked, "Ch-ch-cheese or i-i-i-ice cream?"

Wilson said, "Cheese."

"You know," the voice was gossipy, not imperious for a minute, "F-f-f-f-frank S-s-s-s-swinnerton was here the other day. He said — ice cream!"

Wilson said, "Really? I shouldn't have thought he was that sort of man."

It was like that all through lunch: every remark weighed and weighed again; all the signs secret among the English, the Literati, and the Accepted, were brought out, tested, some found wanting, and some passed, as was the cheese.

At one point, having bullied the absent, there was a shift. It was time, almost formally, to bully Alan Searle.

"My dear," he said, but the phrase was no longer kind, "Alan here knows *everybody* worth knowing. Alan knew Festing Jones!"

I didn't realize that this was supposed to be a joke. I had just been reading Samuel Butler, and Festing Jones was his close friend. I was delighted to be able to talk to Searle. "Did you really?" I said. "Was it true that Butler asked him and another friend to spread his ashes over Lincoln's Inn Fields as a final joke? I see two old men in their top hats, dancing around, strewing ashes."

Maugham was furious, like a child. He commanded a dead silence at the table. Angus Wilson came to the rescue, as he would. "Mary Lee has just had her first book accepted this morning."

"Oh really," voice of ice, "what publisher?"

"Yours." I got my small revenge, fifty years younger than he was, full of martinis, and robbed of Festing Jones.

Hyde Park is just across Park Lane from the Dorchester. I didn't leave. I escaped. All the rest of the daylight I wandered in the park. It was damp, and a mist was in the distance and it smelled of autumn, which is different from our fall—a lying down, no dry wind, no deep frost, damp and dying. I thought of what I had seen and heard of fame, and of that man, who had had so many honors, so much money, and all the public praise that a long career could give him, and who still stammered like a neglected small boy when he was faced with any competition. I saw the face, not as vicious, but as etched with years of pain and bitterness.

"If that is fame I don't ever want it," I told the trees and the martinis and the afternoon.

I knew I couldn't help being an alchemist, transmuting the raw material of life into fiction. It was and is for me a function as obsessive as an oyster making a pearl, an activity that can only be understood by experiencing it, one not to be analyzed by outside observers. But there were things I could help. I could help letting reputation shadow my soul, as Maugham had done; and at the same time, I remembered the kind, gentle man hidden within him that I had seen a few weeks before. I could help being etched as he was by acceptance or denial. I saw that it was not fame itself, but the seeking of fame that could destroy.

I even considered not publishing at all if that was its end. But I rejected that. Not even the martinis or the experience or the cold that was creeping over the park and making me shiver could make that seem anything but self-defeating. We do, as Emily Dickinson said, write our letters to the world, and we want the world to read them.

I had a son to raise, and what money I could glean from the small advances I was condemned to for so long was needed. All this in an afternoon in the park, drunken resolution and paraphrase, swearing on the altar of God eternal vigilance against any form of literary tyranny over my mind.

I vowed to find my energy within and not from reputation, and to avoid the "literary" life. I resolved to be grateful for understanding and praise and honors if they came but never to hang on them, and after finishing the books I would write—how many then I had no idea of—to forget publishing as soon as I could and get back to work.

Now, over thirty years later, and to my shame, a single adverse and smart-aleck review of my book, *Celebration*, by a "remote and ineffectual don" at Oxford, has triggered this recall to warn me once again that I, too, can fall victim to that most familiar of industrial hazards as a writer—literary paranoia. Never mind that the other reviews have been more than favorable. This one thorn sticks, and I must face some regrettable facts before I can pull it out.

Since that fall day in London I have faced the public a dozen times with a book in my hand, as did Rousseau—a gift that I see being thrown over the heads of the reviewers to the people who want to read it, like contraceptives in Dublin airport. Financially, I must stand or fall in the literary industry of New York, as specialized and distilled a center as the diamond and gold merchants who flock together on Forty-seventh Street.

Have I kept the resolutions I made that day? Like New Year's resolutions—only haltingly. Neither the experience I had then, nor any since, has fully armed me for the diminishing act of having to make public a book on which I have spent several private years. Nothing in my necessarily isolated way of living prepares me for the sea change that goes on for a few months, in which I become public, a target and an object, whether I am praised or blamed. The very qualities that make me and most writers what we are also ill fit us for what we have to do.

What I did not know then was that it is the exposure that palls; intelligent praise mitigates it—a godsend, a palliative. We must go through publishing, alas, when we are most vulnerable, bankrupt with fatigue, when we have spent energy deep into our *élan vital* to finish books. Fortunately it only happens once every two or three years. I don't think most of us could stand it oftener. It is more primitive and more frightening than facing the reviewers. But anxiety and fatigue can charge reviewing with more importance than it ought to possess.

I cannot deny that I have gone through all the crises of having to publish, and have been hurt, though never stopped by them. I have had to remind myself over and over that the impetus is outside and predictable: a few real lovers of good writing who read before they judge; a few fine writers who are occasional critics; good luck or bad luck; bad editorial choice of reviewers; professional reviewers with graduate student mentalities who make their livings by "approving of what is approved of" or by grinding abstract axes in public. I have felt their tiny pitons as they climb my back toward their careers. When this happens to me I am tempted by the dying words of Comte, "Only one man ever understood me, and he didn't understand me."

I have hated as much as anyone else being a victim of careless reviewers from the burgeoning academic industry. They remind me of the portrait in *Huckleberry Finn* of the girl who "had two arms folded across her breast, and two arms stretched out in front, and two more reaching up toward the moon." One academic eye is on the book as raw material for acceptable theory. (When I am charged with those twin illusions of MFA programs, point of view and characterization, I feel like I have submitted my book to a "creative writing" workshop in hell.)

Then there is another eye on this year's critical fashion, another eye on The Department, and yet another eye on the Sunday Book Sections or weeklies I call *The Literary Reviews of Tenure*. Alas, having regular jobs and having to publish or perish, they work cheap, and budget-obsessed editors do no honor to writing by overhiring them. By the rules of politeness in publishing, we novelists are supposed to allow ourselves to be used to help others keep their jobs, to be derided, misunderstood, and compared to death without a word of protest.

No writer I know who has achieved a reputation after years of work has escaped having it thrown back in his or her face. I am reminded of the young, poor poets trashing T. S. Eliot in London pubs in the early fifties, or young would-be novelists decrying the reputation of Graham Greene, Henry Green, Somerset Maugham, Angus Wilson, or any other famous writer who had succeeded after long years in that most unforgivable of activities — earning money and critical acceptance.

Alas, I too have been "listed"— that lazy critical habit of making categories instead of reading. There are lists of Southern writers, Jewish writers, Suburban writers, Postmodernists, Minimalists, Maximalists, Premenstrualists, the Sensitive, the Important, and what a friend calls the I'm So Fucking Lonely School of American writing. Finally there are THE GREAT, the list of those who have outlasted their contemporaries, where it helps to be unread, old, male, grouchy, foreign, Eudora Welty, or dead. In the end I say, like the boy in *Zéro de Conduite*, "Monsieur le Professeur, je vous dit merde."

In those few months of public life, we tend to protect ourselves with false nostalgia. Once there were better reviewers. Once there was grace and honor in publishing. This is nonsense. There never was. The marketplace does not change, and Herman Melville still stands awkwardly at literary teas, ignored by Margaret Fuller.

All we ever have had to defend us is time. Time will give the destructive, ambitious critic a footnote, as it did to Lockhart, who was once the feared editor of the *Edinburgh Review*. Now he is mentioned, if at all, because of his advice to the little chemist to go back to his pots — this to John Keats — and his devastating review of *Wuthering Heights*. He has become a bad joke, a parody, a *reductio ad absurdum* of all critics.

Melville died forgotten. Conrad's honors came too late. Faulkner had already been too wounded when long-earned recognition came. When Scott Fitzgerald died, just forty-four years old, people thought he had been dead for years. Poor Stendhal and Melville, dead, provide jobs for academics who act as hatchet men on the living. Few of those we revere now escaped the exhaustion of neglect and denial. I will not be fooled like this. Ataturk once said that there was no such thing as a victim; there were only people who allowed themselves to be victimized.

So, at the age of sixty-eight, I have made myself encounter not only Somerset Maugham and Angus Wilson that day in London thirty-four years ago, but the young writer that I was then, so sure that I would not fall victim to my own weaknesses. The recall of those resolves sustains me, though, and replaces despond with anger if not forgiveness. Better to be sustained by arrogance and curse the night than to yield to mournful self-defense or the bitterness that etched the face of Somerset Maugham.

JEROME BRUNER

Le Patron, Jean Piaget

Piaget asked me whether I enjoyed mountain walking. It was at the end of a day in which Bärbel Inhelder, his longtime associate, and I had been working over the details of some parallel experiments on children's thinking that her students at Geneva and mine at Harvard had been doing. Piaget was not directly involved and had not been with us but, as in everything, his presence was felt. There were differences in interpretation about what the findings signified — important ones — but it had been a friendly day with much joking about the "American" and the "Geneva" way of looking at things. "Le Patron," as Piaget was known half affectionately, half respectfully at his Institute, was on his way home and, as was his custom, had stopped by Bärbel's office to organize the next day's work before starting the half-hour bike ride to his book-crammed house on the outskirts of the city.

As for the invitation, I love walking anywhere, especially in the mountains, and we agreed immediately on an expedition for the next day. Weather permitting, we would cross over to the French side of Lake Geneva, climb the slope of what is referred to locally as "the English Mont Blanc," a gentle alp with good footpaths up one side, and have lunch at a country inn near the top that was accessible by a motor road from the other side. All was agreed upon: it was to be one of those complicated, almost nineteenth-century "outings" that one associates, perhaps, with daguerreotypes and old photo albums.

Le Patron, Bärbel, and I met early the next morning as planned: at the Institut Jean-Jacques Rousseau in the old Palais Wilson on the shore. Prince Vinh Bang, his Vietnamese assistant, an exquisitely handsome and courteous man who looked considerably younger than his years and who dwelled with delicate pleasure on everything Piaget said, was to drive us across the frontier into France to the foot of the mountain, and then drive up the other side of the mountain with his wife to join us for lunch. Vinh Bang was third in succession to his country's throne, Bärbel had told me with a mixture of pride and sadness, for it was the early 1960s and the grinding misery of the civil war and of France's role in it was already becoming apparent in the French-speaking world. But after all, a *prince* . . .

Piaget was waiting, for how long I do not know. When the three of us had taken a train from Geneva to Berne together the year before, we had arrived at the station forty-five minutes early. "He prefers it so," Bärbel had said. This morning he was dressed, as always, in a fusty black suit, a plain white shirt, and a dark tie. The sole sporting elements of his costume were the gray woolen sweater he wore under his jacket and a nondescript rucksack. He was a striking figure — a large head with white hair topped by a country beret that looked as if it had been there forever, an impressive and firm bulk, a striking face of grave intelligence with mirth lines engraved in a rugged peasant complexion. This morning his otherwise achromatic figure was relieved by a single point of vividness: a rosette of the French Legion of Honor glowed on his lapel. When we crossed the border into France, the frontier guard waved us through. "C'est mon passeport, ce petit bouton," he crowed to me, laughing. We soon arrived at the foot of the English Mont Blanc.

Le Patron set a "walker's pace" up the trail: steady, slow, amenable to both easy breathing and easy conversation — a pace for the long haul. The conversation soon became as regular as the walking. It was about the differences between perception and thought, and I recall we were joking about Egon Brunswik's unwillingness to decide whether the nature of perception was cleverly and pragmatically top-down or stupidly and empirically bottom-up.

Then, without a word, Piaget knelt down beside the trail, turned over a rock, and rose with a beautiful snail held triumphantly but delicately between his fingers. He assured me they could always be found there, and Bärbel reminded me that he had spent his youth studying mollusks, especially their form and growth. I laughed and asked him whether his early studies had perhaps predisposed him to a certain preformism in his ideas about growth. Yes, he replied, perhaps, it might have, but rather more toward the view that internal processes prevailed in sorting out the varieties of *aliment* that nourished growth. And then he was back on a theme that we had discussed several times before: he referred to his image of *l'homme calme* and contrasted it to mine of *l'homme agité* — two ways of looking at how man pursues his perceptual life. Do people perceptually highlight certain aspects of the world because they are relevant to transitory and changing needs or do they perceive mainly those stable features that serve the more enduring requirements of species adaptation? We "agreed" that what made perception interesting was that it had to do both—with me holding out for the view that it did neither of them very well, if that's what *he* meant by *agité*.

It was mid-morning. We stopped for a snack in a boulder-strewn meadow about halfway up. Off came his rucksack; out of it came a fresh baguette, a tube of mayonnaise, a head of garlic, a pocket knife, and a garlic press. A beautiful routine began, carried out with the ritual precision of Kabuki theater. A slice of bread was cut, mayonnaise smoothed upon it, and a clove of garlic squeezed on top of that. The garlic and mayonnaise were then delicately mixed and spread. One for Bärbel, one for me, and one for him. I exclaimed with delight that it was the most delicious mountain snack I had ever eaten. He was pleased that I liked it, pleased rather as a priest would be when complimented on the beauties of the Mass by an innocent initiate.

A quarter hour later we were back on the path again, resuming both the pace and the conversation. At the appointed hour we arrived at the inn. The Vinh Bangs were already there and greeted us with a warmth just enough beyond natural courtesy and affection to suggest a certain relief. The meal was jolly, calm, delicious. I wish I could remember the name of the local little wine. It was perfect for the occasion. Piaget said to me: "Le bleu de Bresse est toujours bon ici comme fromage." I ordered some. It too was perfect. We arrived back at the Palais Wilson at 3:45, as planned, and rejoined the assistants. I said to Bärbel that it had been a lovely day. "Yes," she said, "he is an *artiste de la vie*."

POSTSCRIPT

When I finished writing my account of this outing, I sent it to Bärbel Inhelder in Geneva, hoping she would enjoy reading about this day out of memory. And indeed she did, for I soon received a telephone call from her in Geneva, thanking me most warmly for sending it to her. "And by the way . . ."

The conversation that followed, like those at anniversary dinners when family memories are recovered, drew past events out of that historical shadowland where neither epistemology nor ontology entirely rules. Bärbel had telephoned Vinh Bang and they had decided that the outing had occurred in 1957, not in the early 1960s, and that the occasion of my visit was a colloquium on perception that was held at the Institute that summer. The date and the topic seem altogether unlikely to me. But my reasons would not, I am sure, stand up either in a court of law or in a tribunal of historians. How circumstantial am I permitted to be? Were not Bärbel and Prince Vinh Bang carried away by my account of our conversation about Egon Brunswik's theory of perception? Didn't they then wrap a date and event around it to keep it warm and alive?

"Do you remember the wild thunderstorm on the way up, how we got soaked, and how Le Patron had extra, dry clothes in his rucksack that we could all put on? You know, he had everything in that rucksack." Do I remember that thunderstorm? Is it perhaps "represented" in my memory as the "relief" in the expressions of Vinh Bang and his wife when they welcomed us on the verandah of the restaurant? No, I cannot recover the thunderstorm, hard as I may try. I explore my unconscious: Is it that I have Piaget tagged as the "stern father," leaving no room for such nurturant acts as replacing wet clothing with dry?

And suppose I now did a full search of old diaries—suppose, indeed, I *had* old diaries. What would be the status of the entries I might find? Would I find real but forgotten rain and thunder inscribed there? Mary McCarthy's *Memories of a Catholic Girlhood* was published first as fiction—as separate stories—and only later as autobiography. And Paul Valéry once remarked that his most autobiographical poems were those that were unencumbered by memories of the past. What then is an encounter—narrative, autobiography, history, hagiography, anti-hagiography? And what should I make of those aboriginal but forgotten elements of the experience? As a historian I should be delighted to have recovered them. That, after all, is the essence of history.

In the end, I would rather leave the original text unchanged and use a postscript to register the inward nature of what one knows. How I wish there were a counterpart in English for the distinction between *kennen* and *wissen*, *connaître* and *savoir*. For the recalling of an encounter is as surely a creature of autobiographical construction as of historical method.